Cambridge Elements

Elements in Shakespeare and Text
edited by
Claire M. L. Bourne
The Pennsylvania State University
Rory Loughnane
University of Kent

ANNE SHAKESPEARE'S EPITAPH

Katherine West Scheil
University of Minnesota

Shaftesbury Road, Cambridge CB2 8EA, United Kingdom

One Liberty Plaza, 20th Floor, New York, NY 10006, USA

477 Williamstown Road, Port Melbourne, VIC 3207, Australia

314–321, 3rd Floor, Plot 3, Splendor Forum, Jasola District Centre, New Delhi – 110025, India

Cambridge University Press is part of Cambridge University Press & Assessment, a department of the University of Cambridge.

We share the University's mission to contribute to society through the pursuit of education, learning and research at the highest international levels of excellence.

www.cambridge.org
Information on this title: www.cambridge.org/9781009611084

DOI: 10.1017/9781009611091

© Katherine West Scheil 2026

This publication is in copyright. Subject to statutory exception and to the provisions of relevant collective licensing agreements, no reproduction of any part may take place without the written permission of Cambridge University Press & Assessment.

When citing this work, please include a reference to the DOI 10.1017/9781009611091

First published 2026

A catalogue record for this publication is available from the British Library

A Cataloging-in-Publication data record for this Element is available from the Library of Congress

ISBN 978-1-009-61108-4 Paperback
ISSN 2754-4257 (online)
ISSN 2754-4249 (print)

Cambridge University Press & Assessment has no responsibility for the persistence or accuracy of URLs for external or third-party internet websites referred to in this publication and does not guarantee that any content on such websites is, or will remain, accurate or appropriate.

For EU product safety concerns, contact us at Calle de José Abascal, 56, 1°, 28003 Madrid, Spain, or email eugpsr@cambridge.org

Anne Shakespeare's Epitaph

Elements in Shakespeare and Text

DOI: 10.1017/9781009611091
First published online: Feburary 2026

Katherine West Scheil
University of Minnesota

Author for correspondence: Katherine West Scheil, kscheil@umn.edu

ABSTRACT: The Shakespeare family occupies five gravesites on the chancel steps at Holy Trinity Church in Stratford-upon-Avon. Anne Shakespeare's grave is the only one commemorated with a brass plaque and an epitaph in original Latin poetry, eulogizing her as a beloved mother, pious woman, and 'so great a gift'. For nearly four hundred years, this epitaph has remained largely unreadable to visitors, enabling a long history of undervaluing Anne's significant maternal role in the Shakespeare family. *Anne Shakespeare's Epitaph* offers a new reading of the content and the related material conditions and interpersonal connections behind this text. It provides new evidence about the identity of the engraver and suggests several possible scenarios for how the Shakespeare family came to memorialize Anne as a cherished maternal figure. This Element reinscribes the original significance of Anne's epitaph, and reclaims it as an important Shakespearean text that offers traces of a lost documentary record.

KEYWORDS: Shakespeare, Anne Hathaway Shakespeare, Epitaphs, Commemoration, Women

© Katherine West Scheil 2026

ISBNs: 9781009611084 (PB), 9781009611091 (OC)
ISSNs: 2754-4257 (online), 2754-4249 (print)

Contents

Preface: Loss and the Life of Anne Shakespeare   1

Introduction: Anne Shakespeare's Epitaph   9

1   In the Shadow of the Bard: The Dating and Location of Anne Shakespeare's Epitaph   18

2   Materializing Memory: The Production of Anne Shakespeare's Epitaph   30

3   Memorializing the Maternal: Creating the Content of Anne Shakespeare's Epitaph   42

4   Beyond the Words: The Engraver of Anne Shakespeare's Epitaph   61

5   The Epitaph's Geography: Possible London and Stratford-upon-Avon Networks   76

Conclusion: Expanding the World of Anne Shakespeare   104

Appendix: An Edition of Anne Shakespeare's Epitaph   108

Preface: Loss and the Life of Anne Shakespeare

The surviving archival materials related to Anne Shakespeare are scant.[1] Her epitaph in Holy Trinity Church in Stratford-upon-Avon (the subject of this Element) tells us that she died on 6 August 1623 at the age of sixty-seven. From this, we can infer that she was born in 1556, though no documentary records remain for her birth. Her Shottery family home of Hewlands, now Anne Hathaway's Cottage, survives, but we do not know when Anne lived there, for how long, or under what circumstances.[2] Her father's will of 1581 names her as 'Agnes', and the 1601 will of the Hathaway family shepherd, Thomas Whittington, refers to 'Anne Shaxpere wyffe unto Mr Wyyam Shaxspere' and entrusts her with money 'for the poore people of Stratford' in her 'hand'.[3] Anne's epitaph also names her as the 'wife of William Shakespeare', and two documents related to her marriage survive: the marriage licence and the marriage bond, both from November 1582. In Shakespeare's will of 1616, as 'my wyf', she is given 'my second best bed with the furniture', and the parish register of Stratford-upon-Avon for her burial lists her as 'Mrs. Shakspeare'. The aforelisted items provide an incomplete picture of the life of Anne Shakespeare, and we cannot assume that this is a full account of all the documents related to her that may once have existed, or that her life has been adequately captured in documentary form. Further, several of these surviving documents have been fetishized, particularly Shakespeare's will, to the point of dominating

---

[1] I provide a list of surviving archival documents for Anne Shakespeare in Appendix 1 of *Imagining Shakespeare's Wife: The Afterlife of Anne Hathaway* (Cambridge: Cambridge University Press, 2018), and in my *Oxford Dictionary of National Biography* entry on Anne ('Hathaway [married name Shakespeare], Anne [c.1555/56–1623], wife of William Shakespeare', *Oxford Dictionary of National Biography*, 12 August 2021). A longer discussion of these documents appears in *Imagining Shakespeare's Wife*, 3–18.

[2] I refer to Anne by her first name rather than surname, to avoid confusion with William Shakespeare, most commonly referred to by his surname.

[3] Robert Bearman, 'Thomas Whittington Includes in His Will a Debt', https://shakespearedocumented.folger.edu/resource/document/thomas-whittington-includes-his-will-debt-owing-him-40-shillings-hand-anne.

depictions of Anne that have endured for centuries but are built on piecemeal evidence.

Another complication to Anne's incomplete archive is the fact that all of these documents have come to light at staggered times over the last four centuries. Anne's epitaph was the earliest recorded piece of evidence about her life, with a transcription first appearing as early as July of 1634 in the manuscript notes of William Dugdale.[4] Shakespeare's will was discovered in 1747, the marriage licence bond in 1836, and the registry entry for the marriage in 1880. Matthew Steggle has recently made a persuasive case for an additional document that locates Anne Shakespeare with her husband in London around 1599–1603 and may offer evidence of her literacy (as discussed later in this Element). Steggle's account of the provenance of this letter fragment illustrates how precarious the evidence about early modern subjects, especially women, can be and how easily it can become lost. The fragment of a letter addressed to 'Mrs Shakspaire' was bound in another book printed by Stratfordian and Londoner Richard Field likely from 1608. It somehow ended up near the Welsh border in Lady Hawkins' School in Kington, Herefordshire, where it remained until 1978, when it was donated to Hereford Cathedral Library. The fragment was first discovered during cataloguing in 1978 by Honorary Cathedral Librarian F. C. Morgan, who had just turned 100. Morgan published a brief (and posthumous) account of the letter in *Notes and Queries*, with the cryptic title of 'Honorificabilitudinitatibus', which gives no indication of the subject of the piece, perhaps explaining the lack of scholarly attention it has received.[5] Only through Steggle's reassessment of this document has its potential significance been brought to light, and along with it, a reminder of the instability of the archive related to Anne Shakespeare.[6]

---

[4] See Tom Reedy, 'William Dugdale on Shakespeare and His Monument', *Shakespeare Quarterly* 66.2 (2015): 188–96. Dugdale's draft manuscript is held in the ancestral library at Merevale Hall.

[5] Frederick Charles Morgan, 'Honorificabilitudinitatibus', *Notes and Queries* 25.5 (1978): 445.

[6] Matthew Steggle, 'The Shakspaires of Trinity Lane: A Possible Shakespeare Life-Record', *Shakespeare* 21.2 (2025): 450–94.

Other than the items listed earlier, no other papers connected to Anne Shakespeare have been identified to date – no diary, books, correspondence, or legal cases. That does not mean that such items never existed, and absence of evidence is not necessarily negative evidence. In fact, one account (discussed in more depth later in this Element) suggests that there *were* books and other papers in New Place, Anne's home in Stratford-upon-Avon from 1597 to 1623, which were seized in 1637 and which may have provided a fuller picture of her life. Incomplete surviving evidence does not mean that her story cannot be told, though it is important not to construct her life story based only on the materials that survive about her without acknowledging what has been lost or never recorded in the first place.[7] There are many aspects of Anne Shakespeare's life for which we have no documentary evidence, so any narrative about her life must rely on an incomplete archive. The results have often been seemingly authoritative accounts that are actually built on shaky ground.

So how does one go about telling the stories of historical figures for whom we have an incomplete archive, and for whom any life narrative relies on fragmentary evidence? One option is not to tell the story at all, given that conjecture, hypothetical scenarios, and suggestive ideas have to be used out of necessity, in order to fill in the gaps. Another option is to refuse to enhance surviving factual information, but then these lives – mainly of women – remain stagnant, trapped in the narrow matrix of extant documents in the mode of 'cabbage that has been reboiled a thousand times',

---

[7] Recent works on documentary loss in the early modern field have been helpful in thinking about Anne's lost archive, especially Roslyn L. Knutson, David McInnis, and Matthew Steggle, *Loss and the Literary Culture of Shakespeare's Time* (Cham: Springer International, 2020); and David McInnis, *Shakespeare and Lost Plays: Reimagining Drama in Early Modern England* (Cambridge: Cambridge University Press, 2021). As Robert Bearman puts it, 'many of the documents relating to events that happened 400 years ago have, "ephemeral" or not, come down to us simply by chance', and what has survived is a 'motley collection of material'. 'What Is an "Ephemeral Archive"? Stratford-upon-Avon, 1550–1650: A Case Study', in *Practices of Ephemera in Early Modern England*, eds. Callan Davies, Hannah Lilley, and Catherine Richardson (New York: Routledge, 2023), 65–82.

as Daniel Wyttenbach put it.⁸ Or, even worse, the lives of women become subservient to whatever narrative best serves their male counterparts. This has been the case with Anne Shakespeare, whose life has frequently been entrenched in prejudicial, misogynist narratives that have ossified into facts in order to make particular arguments about Shakespeare.

The absence of evidence about Anne's life has usually not worked in her favour, for reasons I have outlined elsewhere, and in both fictional works and biographies (sometimes one and the same) she has often occupied a stereotypically negative role as a predatory older woman who entrapped a young Shakespeare.⁹ The version of Anne Shakespeare as both a shrew and a mistake is deeply entrenched, and a few instances should suffice. Frank Harris, in his 1910 book *The Women of Shakespeare*, describes Anne as a 'jealous scolding shrew wife' to whom Shakespeare 'crept home to Stratford' to die, and who should be jettisoned to 'the lowest hell of jealousy, rage and humiliation'.¹⁰ The Anne that James Joyce creates in Book 9 of *Ulysses* is a haunting portrait of an elderly, haggard Anne even more lurid than in Harris's version: 'And in New Place a slack dishonoured body that once was comely, once as sweet, as fresh as cinnamon, now her leaves falling, all bare, frighted of the narrow grave and unforgiven.' She is 'the ugliest doxy in all Warwickshire' and 'a boldfaced Stratford wench who tumbles in a cornfield a lover younger than herself'.¹¹ Likewise, Anthony Burgess's Anne in his 1964 novel *Nothing Like the Sun*, is a wife for whom Shakespeare felt 'hatred ... like black vomit' and 'a great rage which justifies murder', a 'groaning old croan [going] about her housewifely tasks, busying herself with the making of sick man's broth' who would 'sit scratching her spent loins through

---

⁸ Daniel Wyttenback, *Bibliotheca Critica*, vol.3, part 3 (Amsterdam, 1808), 48. Knutson, McInnis, and Steggle use this phrase in their introduction to *Loss and the Literary Culture of Shakespeare's Time*, 1.

⁹ See *Imagining Shakespeare's Wife*, especially xiii–xxiii.

¹⁰ Frank Harris, *The Women of Shakespeare* (London: Methuen, 1911), x–xi, 22, 266.

¹¹ James Joyce, *Ulysses*, ed. Hans Walter Gabler (New York: Vintage Books, 1986), 166, 156–7, 159.

her kirtle, mumbling her book'.[12] More recently, primarily in a chapter entitled 'Wooing, Wedding, and Repenting', Stephen Greenblatt unambiguously proclaims in his biography *Will in the World: How Shakespeare Became Shakespeare* (2004, reissued in 2016) that Shakespeare wanted to abandon his 'disastrous mistake' of a wife; he was 'dragged to the altar' for a marriage that was 'doomed from the start'; he viewed Anne with 'contempt' and 'sour anger'; and had a 'strange ineradicable distaste for her that he felt deep within him'. Though this Shakespeare feared the charnel house, claims Greenblatt, 'he may have feared still more that one day his grave would be opened to let in the body of Anne Shakespeare'.[13] This influential denigration of Anne has circulated for twenty years and remains widely available in print.[14] Yet this 'Anne' is only possible if one uses selective evidence and ignores the subject of this Element – Anne Shakespeare's epitaph – which Greenblatt dismisses as a 'strange inscription'.[15]

In scholarly discussions of her life, Anne's epitaph has been significantly underplayed. Most accounts of Anne are found within biographies of Shakespeare, where she is conscripted to serve a role in his life story.[16] Further, biographies of Shakespeare rarely extend past his death in 1616, which has resulted in much greater emphasis on the biographical pieces of Anne's life during Shakespeare's lifetime – the courtship, marriage, and Shakespeare's will – and very little mention of the life she led after he died and, of course, her epitaph.[17] Katherine Duncan-Jones sees Anne as part of

[12] Anthony Burgess, *Nothing Like the Sun: A Story of Shakespeare's Love Life* (New York: W.W. Norton, 1964), 42–43, 30, 191, 31.

[13] Stephen Greenblatt, *Will in the World: How Shakespeare Became Shakespeare* (New York: W.W. Norton, 2004, 2016), 140, 124, 141, 123, 387, 145, 148.

[14] As late as 2021, Greenblatt still claimed that the Shakespeares' relationship was a 'moribund marriage' ('A Wisewoman in Stratford: A Review of *Hamnet*', *The New York Review of Books* [14 January 2021]: 16).

[15] Greenblatt, *Will in the World*, 315.

[16] For an extended discussion of Anne in biographies of Shakespeare, see *Imagining Shakespeare's Wife*, 153–69.

[17] James O. Halliwell [Phillips] includes a replica of the brass plaque but no analysis in *The Works of William Shakespeare*, vol. 1 (London: C. and J. Adlard, 1853),

Shakespeare's 'sowing wild oats' and the outlet for his 'uncontrollable surges of testosterone', with no mention of her epitaph, perhaps understandably given her depiction.[18] Jonathan Bate likewise omits Anne's epitaph from his biography *Soul of the Age: A Biography of the Mind of William Shakespeare* (2009), focusing instead on Anne's role in the Shakespeare marriage.[19] René Weis contends that both William and Anne were unfaithful, and includes a brief mention of her epitaph as a reaction to Shakespeare's adultery, from her daughters who 'obviously adored her and probably suspected that she had suffered from their father's infidelities and prolonged absences in London'.[20] Two more recent biographies, by Lois Potter and Paul Menzer, only briefly mention Anne's epitaph.[21] The most detailed discussion of Anne's epitaph to date is not in a work about Anne or in a biography, but rather in Benjamin Roland Lewis's 1940 collection of Shakespeare-related documents. Lewis provides a detailed transcription and brief analysis of content, referring to the epitaph as a testimony that 'speaks directly and intimately as of a heartbroken daughter to a departed loved mother'.[22]

254–5. Joseph Quincy Adams includes Anne's epitaph with a translation, but no commentary (*A Life of William Shakespeare* [Boston: Houghton Mifflin, 1925], 481–2). Edgar I. Fripp, in his *Shakespeare Man and Artist*, reproduces the full engraving on the brass plaque, including the decorative details but does not comment on the contents except to say 'the grief is Susana's, the Latin, probably, Doctor Hall's' ([Oxford: Oxford University Press, 1938], 2: 853–4).

[18] Katherine Duncan-Jones, *Ungentle Shakespeare: Scenes from His Life* (London: Arden, 2001), 17.

[19] Jonathan Bate, *Soul of the Age: A Biography of the Mind of William Shakespeare* (London: Viking, 2008).

[20] 'That Shakespeare committed adultery while he was in London is scarcely in doubt; that in his turn he might have been cheated on in Stratford during his long absences, and perhaps by a wayward brother, should not be ruled out' (René Weis, *Shakespeare Revealed: A Biography* [London: John Murray, 2007], 276, 370–1).

[21] Lois Potter, *The Life of William Shakespeare: A Critical Biography* (Malden: Wiley-Blackwell, 2012); and Paul Menzer, *William Shakespeare: A Brief Life* (London: Wiley-Blackwell, 2023).

[22] B. Roland Lewis, *The Shakespeare Documents: Facsimiles, Transliterations, Translations, and Commentary* (Stanford: Stanford University Press, 1940), 580–3.

The only full-length biography of Anne is Germaine Greer's *Shakespeare's Wife* (2007). As her title suggests, Greer's focus is on Anne's role as a wife, and the epitaph only makes a few brief appearances. Greer provides a translation of the Latin section but includes no extended analysis or commentary on the content.[23] My biographical chapter on Anne in *The Shakespeare Circle* (2016) sets out the array of surviving facts about her, with a section on her epitaph and a brief analysis of the content. Lena Cowen Orlin gives Anne's epitaph attention in *The Private Life of William Shakespeare* (2021), focusing mainly on possible dating inaccuracies related to her birth year, which the epitaph helps to establish.[24] Only in 2021 did Anne receive her own entry (including a section dedicated to her epitaph) in the *Oxford Dictionary of National Biography*, where previously she had been subsumed under Shakespeare's entry.[25] Until now, no full-length study of Anne's epitaph has existed, let alone told the story of her life through its text and contexts.

This Element puts Anne Shakespeare's epitaph centre stage for the first time and explores what we might be able to learn by looking closely at the material conditions, the personal connections, and the literary networks behind the epitaph's creation, and using these newly illuminated interrelations to interpret her life. I attempt to reconstruct the circumstances that led to the planning, creation, and production of Anne's epitaph, based on common practice, similar surviving historical documents, and creative but plausible ways to flesh out historical details. Anne's epitaph is particularly important for adding new emphasis to Anne as a mother, a role that her daughters deliberately chose as the 'Anne' they wanted to immortalize for posterity. This maternal 'Anne' complements facets of her life that have been explored by other scholars, including Anne as a businesswoman by Lena Cowen Orlin, and Anne as a cohabitant with her husband, sharing business and social acquaintances in London, by Matthew Steggle.[26]

---

[23] Germaine Greer, *Shakespeare's Wife* (London: Bloomsbury, 2007), 343.

[24] Lena Orlin, *The Private Life of William Shakespeare* (Oxford: Oxford University Press, 2021), 76–78.

[25] Scheil, 'Hathaway [married name Shakespeare], Anne'.

[26] Lena Orlin, 'Anne by Indirection', *Shakespeare Quarterly* 65.4 (2014): 421–54; Steggle, 'The Shakspaires of Trinity Lane'.

My approach employs a speculative methodology, drawing from innovative Shakespeare studies, to examine the potential ramifications associated with the material conditions of Anne's epitaph. Orlin uses a methodology of cognate lives to suggest missing archival documents in her *Shakespeare Quarterly* article 'Anne by Indirection', where the life of Elizabeth Quiney provides a possible context for Anne Shakespeare and is used to suggest missing archival documents. Likewise, in *The Private Life of William Shakespeare*, Orlin relies on parallel lives to offer analogies that might help explain biographical cruxes where further details are missing. Similarly, Geoffrey Marsh, in *Living With Shakespeare* uses parishioners in St. Helen's Bishopsgate to provide context for some of the individuals whose lives may have intersected with Shakespeare's own, but for which there is no documentary evidence of direct connections. Marsh describes his method as putting 'some probable flesh on the bare bones of events largely based on fragmentary official records'. Paul Edmondson and Stanley Wells, editors of *The Shakespeare Circle*, underline the need to imaginatively go 'beyond narrowly documented evidence' in order to open up new possibilities about lives for which an incomplete archive survives.[27] Roslyn L. Knutson, David McInnis, and Matthew Steggle's collection *Loss and the Literary Culture of Shakespeare's Time* offers an additional methodological model for how to responsibly carry out work when 'lostness in a plurality of forms' permeates the field.[28]

In *Anne Shakespeare's Epitaph*, I offer a way to rewrite Anne's maternal history through a 'Shakespearean text' that I will suggest originates from the Shakespeare women, and that was also linked to social networks that situate Anne and her legacy in a new context, one related to but also distinct from her husband. In so doing, I imagine lost archival documents that may

---

[27] Orlin, 'Anne by Indirection', and *The Private Life of William Shakespeare* (Oxford: Oxford University Press, 2021); Geoffrey Marsh, *Living with Shakespeare: St. Helen's Parish, London, 1593–1598* (Edinburgh: Edinburgh University Press, 2021), 15; Paul Edmondson and Stanley Wells, eds., *The Shakespeare Circle* (Cambridge: Cambridge University Press, 2016).

[28] Knutson, McInnis, and Steggle, *Loss and the Literary Culture of Shakespeare's Time*, 2.

have once existed, in order to increase the possible footprint of Anne
Shakespeare's life. I offer multiple interpretations and scenarios for the
stories that these documents might tell, with as much transparency as
possible in terms of likelihood and responsible disclosure of tentative
evidence. Particularly in the last section of this Element, I resist the urge
to tell a single narrative about how Anne's life came to be commemorated in
her epitaph, choosing instead to offer multiple scenarios, many of which
have an equal probability of being 'true'. I hope my deliberate reluctance to
make a definitive pronouncement where there is insufficient and fragmentary evidence will encourage others to think outside the box, to hold
multiple 'Annes' in their imaginations at once, and to avoid imposing
a single narrative on a life where multiple possibilities are equally plausible.

Introduction: Anne Shakespeare's Epitaph

> Among all funeral honours Epitaphes have alwaies bene most respective,
> for in them love was shewed to the deceased, memory was continued to
> posterity, friends were comforted, and the reader put in mind of humane
> frailty. William Camden, *Remains Concerning Britain* (1605)

Nestled on the banks of the River Avon in the medieval market town of
Stratford-upon-Avon, Holy Trinity Church occupies a site that has been
a place of worship since the ninth century. As the oldest building in
Stratford, the present structure dates from 1210 and attracts thousands of
tourists, mainly to pay homage to the most famous resident of the town –
William Shakespeare – who is buried there on the chancel steps. Built in the
late 1400s, the chancel is the most sacred part of the church, and the first
grave on the north end of chancel steps is not that of William Shakespeare,
but rather, his wife Anne Shakespeare. The epitaph on Anne's memorial
brass plaque, honouring her in original Latin poetry as a beloved mother
and 'so great a gift', has been there for nearly 400 years. It has remained in
place just steps from where Anne worshiped with her family and where her
three children were baptized, and not far from where she buried her only
son Hamnet in the churchyard in 1596. Anne's grave occupies the place

where she bade farewell to her famous husband seven years before her own death, and would have returned to honour his memory, possibly thinking about her own mortality and when she would occupy the empty space reserved for her next to his grave.

Anne Shakespeare's brass epitaph has weathered the footsteps of thousands of pilgrims seeking out her husband's grave and monument, many of whom often stood on her grave for the best view. It survived the conflict of the English Civil War in Stratford; it outlasted Anne's home of New Place, destroyed in 1759, where she spent the last quarter-century of her life; it has endured longer than the church's charnel house (torn down in 1800) that Shakespeare warned against in the curse on his grave. Anne's epitaph was there when American Delia Bacon travelled to Stratford in 1856, planning to break into Shakespeare's grave to find the secrets to his supposed collaborative authorship. It was there when the fifty-six suffragettes visited Holy Trinity Church in 1913 before holding a public meeting in Rother Market. It was there when 40 local soldiers married in the church between 1917 and 1918, and when Stratford's mothers and widows buried the 235 soldiers lost in the Great War. Anne's epitaph was there when a German reconnaissance plane flew over Stratford-upon-Avon in July 1940, photographing potential targets including the bridges over the River Avon. It was there when another set of mothers and widows mourned the sons of Stratford who did not return from that war and are commemorated nearby in the church. It was there in 2022 when carvings of Anne and William Shakespeare were added to the north transept window and when novelist Maggie O'Farrell dedicated two rowan trees to Anne's twin children in the churchyard. Nearly 400 years of social upheaval, war, baptisms, marriages, funerals, and the foot traffic of thousands of tourists and local parishioners, have left nary a mark on Anne's grave. Its 'characters of brass' have withstood 'the tooth of time' and the 'razure of oblivion', as one notable contemporary put it.[29]

---

[29] William Shakespeare, *Measure for Measure*, 5.1.11–13. Unless otherwise noted, all citations from Shakespeare's works are from *The New Oxford Shakespeare: Modern Critical Edition*, ed. Gary Taylor, John Jowett, Terri Bourus, and Gabriel Egan (Oxford: Oxford University Press, 2016).

Anne's epitaph, likely planned by her two daughters (as I discuss later), was created from the most permanent material available – commemorative brass – in hopes that their praise of her as a mother would outlast generations and serve as an inspiration in a prominent part of the parish church, perhaps inspired by their father's verses in Sonnet 81:

> Your monument shall be my gentle verse,
> Which eyes not yet created shall o'er-read,
> And tongues to be your being shall rehearse,
> When all the breathers of this world are dead.
> You still shall live ...

While Anne's epitaph itself 'still lives' in pristine condition, its content has not been readily available to visitors, visible for the most part only in the outline of a brass plaque on a stone slab between the grave and monument of her famous husband. After the altar rail was moved in front of the Shakespeare graves in the nineteenth century, it became even more difficult to decipher Anne's epitaph, since the wording would be upside down for viewers who now had to stand behind the altar rail, and the Latin section was untranslated.[30] An English translation was not publicly accessible at Holy Trinity in any permanent display until the spring of 2023, when a loose laminated sheet was made available for visitors.[31] This epitaph is the most reliable piece of evidence about Anne's life, and its relative

---

[30] One visitor in 1885 remarked that since the altar rail was put up, 'as the slabs of the Shakespeare family lie so that their letters are upside down to the gaze of the public, they might easily escape notice, were it not for the paid attendant, who leads the visitor up, and spreads upon the slab a "rubbing" of the words, that he may read' (E. Poingdestre, 'A Summer Day at Stratford-on-Avon', *Frank Leslie's Popular Monthly* 20.4 [October 1885]: 411).

[31] An 1892 photo in the Shakespeare Birthplace Trust Archives shows a transcription of Anne's epitaph placed on the floor next to the brass plaque but not within a readable distance from the altar rail (SC 4/37/11). Beginning in the 1840s, income from visitors to the Shakespeare graves in Holy Trinity was both welcome and vital to the church's financial health (Mairi Macdonald, '"Not a Memorial to Shakespeare, but a Place for Divine Worship": The Vicars of

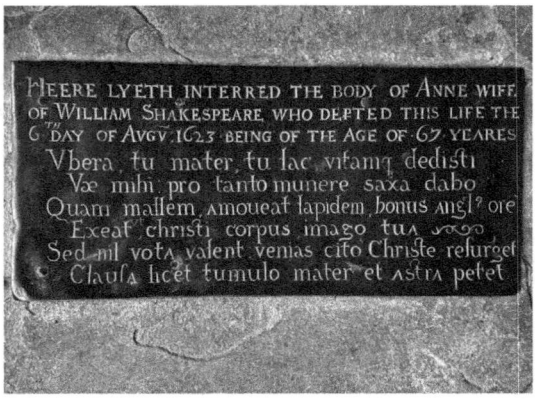

Figure 1 Anne Shakespeare's epitaph, Holy Trinity Church, Stratford-upon-Avon (author's own photo)

obscurity has had a substantial effect on her afterlife, enabling a long history of dismissal and erasure of the important maternal role she played in the Shakespeare family and in her community.

Anne's is the only Shakespeare family grave commemorated with a memorial brass.[32] It features an English section of basic biographical information, and a Latin section of original poetry eulogizing her as a beloved mother and 'so great a gift' (Figure 1). In translation, the Latin part reads:

> You, Mother, gave [your] breasts, milk, and life;
> Woe is me: in return for so great a gift I shall give rocks

Stratford and the Shakespeare Phenomenon, 1616–1964', *Warwickshire History* 11.6 [2001/2002]: 207–226).

[32] The term 'memorial brass' refers to 'any inscription, figure, shield of arms or other device engraved for commemorative purpose in flat sheet "brass"', and the form dates from the thirteenth century in England. See Malcolm Norris, *Monumental Brasses: The Craft* (London: Faber and Faber, 1978), 23.

> How I'd prefer, I would pray, that the good angel should move the stone away
>
> [And] out would come, like the body of Christ, the image of you!
> But prayers are of no avail: come quickly, Christ, she shall rise again
> [My] mother, although she has been shut in the tomb, and she shall seek the stars.[33]

As a memorial designed to carry 'the story of someone's past far into the future', the 'story' of Anne immortalized on her epitaph has been suppressed and even, in some cases, erased from history.[34] Throughout the seventeenth and eighteenth centuries, Holy Trinity was the top destination for tourists in Stratford, but no visitor other than William Dugdale (discussed in more detail later in this Element) remarked on Anne's grave.[35] John Dowdall, in a letter to a Mr. Southwell dated 10 April 1693, remarks on Shakespeare's monument and transcribes its inscription as well as the curse on Shakespeare's grave, but does not mention Anne's epitaph.[36] Likewise,

---

[33] I am grateful to Victoria Moul for extensive consultation on the transcription and translation of Anne's epitaph and on the context for early modern Latin. Other recent translations of Anne's epitaph include Val Horsler's in *Shakespeare's Church* (London: Third Millennium 2010), 81; and Chris Laoutaris's in *Shakespeare's Book: The Intertwined Lives behind the First Folio* (London: William Collins, 2023), 257.

[34] Peter Ross, *A Tomb with a View: The Stories and Glories of Graveyards* (London: Headline, 2020), 49.

[35] Dugdale copied the wording in his manuscript notes, likely from July of 1634, and Anne's epitaph appears in his *The Antiquities of Warwickshire, Illustrated* (London: Thomas Warren, 1656), 518.

[36] Letter signed from John Dowdall, Butler's Marston, Warwickshire, to Mr. Southwell, 10 April 1693, fols 3v-4r, V.a.74, Folger Shakespeare Library. Other early visitors who mention William Shakespeare's grave and/or monument but ignore Anne's include a Lieutenant Hammond in August of 1634 (MS Lansdowne 213, fol. 332v, British Library); Francis Fane in his commonplace books of 1655 and 1672; and Henry Newcombe in his 1669 commonplace book. See Jean L. Wilson, 'The Ledger to Mary Jackson (d. Jan. 20 1676) at Allesley, Warwickshire, and the Grave of William Shakespeare', *Church Monuments*

William Hall in 1694 copied Shakespeare's epitaph and commented on his monument in a letter to his friend Edward Thwaites, likely standing on Anne's grave in order to see it from the best angle, since the altar rail was behind the Shakespeare family graves at the time.[37] Hall makes no mention of Anne's brass epitaph which was also there. When actor Thomas Betterton visited Holy Trinity Church to look at parish documents for Nicholas Rowe's 1709 biography, he would have seen Anne's epitaph, but Rowe's biography does not include any information that Betterton could have gleaned from Anne's grave. Within a hundred years of her death, the details of Anne's life recorded on her epitaph had already receded from view, even though the record of her as a beloved mother remained in its original place.

Early illustrators of Holy Trinity Church were similarly dismissive of Anne's epitaph. The engraver George Vertue replaced Anne's epitaph in his 1737 sketch of the Holy Trinity chancel with the single word 'wife' (Figure 2) and depicted a figure standing on Anne's grave to get a better view of Shakespeare's monument. By 1795, Samuel Ireland erased Anne's grave entirely in his drawing of 'Shakspeare's Monument', supplanting it with an enlarged rotated version of Shakespeare's grave (Figure 3).

These early omissions and erasures of Anne's epitaph parallel the ways she has frequently been imagined in her afterlife, by both biographers and other writers seeking to create a particular 'Shakespeare' by manipulating the few surviving details of Anne's life, as if her only purpose was to shed light on her famous husband. Most of these ill-founded narratives emerge from neglect of her epitaph, from misreadings of the 'second best bed' bequest in Shakespeare's will, from the age difference between the Shakespeares, and from a desire to create an urban-based libertine Shakespeare rather than a happily married domestic father of three children

Society (April 2016), https://churchmonumentssociety.org/monument-of-the-month/the-ledger-to-mary-jackson-d-jan-20-1676-at-allesley-warwickshire-and-the-grave-of-william-shakespeare.

[37] William Hall to Edward Thwaites, 1694, MS Rawlinson D. 377, fol. 90, Bodleian Library.

Figure 2 George Vertue's sketch of the Shakespeare monument, 1737. From the British Library Collection, Add MS 70438, fol. 17.

from Warwickshire. One of the earliest commentators on Anne's epitaph, editor Edmond Malone, recorded the English text on the plaque (published posthumously in 1821), and then declared, 'after this inscription follow six Latin verses not worth preserving'.[38] Malone's Shakespeare-centric bias has contributed to long-standing neglect of a fundamental piece of evidence about Anne. By expunging a key passage of Anne's epitaph, Malone's denigration marks a persistent history of misogynist accounts of her life. Biographers and writers, driven by desire for a particular version of

---

[38] Edmond Malone, *The Plays and Poems of William Shakespeare, with the Corrections and Illustrations of Various Commentators* (London: F.C. and J. Rivington, 1821), 2:616.

Figure 3 'Shakspeare's Monument', from Samuel Ireland, *Picturesque Views on the Upper, or Warwickshire Avon*, 1795. Image courtesy of the Folger Shakespeare Library, ART File S527.2 no.155a

'Shakespeare', have often ignored or obscured Anne's daughters' poetic immortalization of her.

In *Anne Shakespeare's Epitaph*, I propose new readings both of the content of Anne Shakespeare's epitaph and of the material conditions that produced it – how it was made, why it was created, and by whom – in order to give this key piece of evidence new prominence in Anne's story. I begin by showing that Anne Shakespeare's death was not given short shrift with a *pro forma* boilerplate marker from a local hack engraver, for a woman who was best forgotten. On the contrary, her family (namely her daughters Susanna and Judith) honoured her as 'so great a gift' by paying for a burial on the chancel steps, the 'liturgical heart' of Holy Trinity Church;[39] composing original Latin poetry; and, as I suggest later, commissioning one of the most prominent London engravers to memorialize her in the more permanent form of brass. These were acts of remembrance that went well beyond the basics of minimal commemorative practices. I offer new evidence about the identity of the engraver of Anne's epitaph, linking her in new ways to the literary world of London, and I suggest several possible scenarios for how the Shakespeare family came to memorialize this beloved wife, mother, grandmother, and woman. *Anne Shakespeare's Epitaph* thus reinscribes the importance that this memorial held when it was commissioned, created, and put into place in what Peter Sherlock calls a 'living site of memory'.[40] In doing so, this study suggests a much richer potential life for Anne by reclaiming the epitaph as an important 'Shakespearean text' from the Shakespeare family women, largely hidden in plain sight for nearly 400 years.[41]

This Element isn't merely about a forgotten brass plaque in a Warwickshire parish church. It is also a story about how Anne Shakespeare, wife to one of history's most famous men, was enduringly memorialized *not* as a wife but instead as a mother by her own daughters, Susanna Shakespeare Hall and Judith Shakespeare Quiney, who were both mothers at the time. This Element explores the legacy of that maternal memorial through generations of dismissal and suppression. In what we would recognize as a feminist statement, Susanna and Judith boldly asserted the significance of motherhood on a par with their iconic father's literary legacy.

---

[39] Warwick Rodwell, *The Archaeology of Churches* (Stroud: Amberley, 2012), 72.

[40] Peter Sherlock, *Monuments and Memory in Early Modern England* (Aldershot: Ashgate, 2008), 210.

[41] Claiming Anne's epitaph as a text by the surviving Shakespeare women resonates with Matthew Steggle's attribution of the 'Spiritual Testament' to Joan Shakespeare Hart, who as he points out, 'despite being the sister of the most famous writer in Western history', has been 'almost unknown'. See 'John Shakespeare's "Spiritual Testament" Is Not John Shakespeare's', *Shakespeare Quarterly* 75.1 (2024): 70–71 and his forthcoming Element in this series.

1 In the Shadow of the Bard: The Dating and Location of Anne Shakespeare's Epitaph

Both the date and the location of Anne's epitaph can offer clues about her life. As I will argue, the epitaph was created within roughly a decade of her death and installed in a space that would have been notable in her community. Anne Shakespeare died at age sixty-seven on 6 August 1623, was named in the parish register of Stratford-upon-Avon as 'Mrs. Shakspeare', and was buried on 8 August in a well-chosen and significant location.[42] Her grave is positioned in the shadow of Shakespeare's funerary monument (on the north wall of the chancel) and next to his grave, on his left side. When Anne died, Shakespeare's grave and his wall monument would have already been in place; Leonard Digges refers to 'thy Stratford moniment' in his dedication to the 1623 First Folio.[43] Because Anne's grave is placed between Shakespeare's grave and his monument, it is likely that the space to Shakespeare's left (as was tradition) was reserved for Anne before Shakespeare was buried; otherwise, it would have made more sense for his grave to be next to his monument rather than separated by the burial space for Anne.[44] The graves of Anne and William Shakespeare are

---

[42] Robert Bearman observes that Anne's 'superior social status is indicated by the term "M^{rs}" for "Mistress" instead of the term "widow" which was used in most other cases, including that of Shakespeare's mother's burial' ('Parish register entry recording Anne Hathaway Shakespeare's burial', *Shakespeare Documented*, https://doi.org/10.37078/437). The registry at Worcester lists her as 'Mrs Ann Shakespeare'.

[43] Leonard Digges, 'To the Memorie of the Deceased Author Maister W. Shakesepeare', in *Mr. William Shakespeares Comedies, Histories, & Tragedies* (London: Edward Blount et al., 1623), sig. πA5. See Robert Bearman, 'The Shakespeare Family Ledger Stones in Holy Trinity Church, Stratford-upon-Avon', *Unpublished Documentary Report for the Parochial Church Council* (2014): 33–34. Mairi Macdonald suggests that Shakespeare's monument may have been in place as early as May of 1619, before Thomas Wilson became vicar, because he likely would not have been in favour of an elaborate monument ('Not a Memorial to Shakespeare', 207).

[44] Orlin, *Private Life*, 218. Sarah Tarlow points out that 'the place of the body was important not only in relation to the sacred geography of an area but also in relation to its social geography' (*Ritual, Belief and the Dead in Early Modern*

Figure 4 The Shakespeare Family Graves (Anne Shakespeare, William Shakespeare, Thomas Nash, John Hall, Susanna Shakespeare Hall), Holy Trinity Church, Stratford-upon-Avon (author's own photo)

shallower than the other three family graves on the chancel steps, which also suggests that they may have been planned together as a unit.[45]

Anne was the first family member to be interred after Shakespeare, and the location of her grave established the chancel steps as a family burial plot rather than simply the site of Shakespeare's grave (Figure 4). As Erica Carrick Utsi and Kevin Colls point out, '[T]he fact that the Shakespeare graves exist in an unbroken line is not merely a reflection of William Shakespeare's investment in Chancel privileges in 1605 but also implies

---

Britain and Ireland [Cambridge: Cambridge University Press, 2011], 108). Other Hathaway family graves are recorded with inscriptions elsewhere on the floor of the church but not the chancel. See Rowland Freeman, *A Brief Account of Stratford-upon-Avon, with a Particular Description and Survey of the Collegiate Church, etc.* (Stratford: E. Walford, 1800), 55, 68.

[45] Erica Carrick Utsi and Kevin S. Colls, 'The GPR Investigation of the Shakespeare Family Graves', *Archaeological Prospection* 24 (2017): 349, 351.

immense and enduring respect for him and for his family'.[46] The most desirable place for burial in a church was near the altar, and the chancel would have been the most expensive burial space.[47] Recent archaeological research has discovered that the Shakespeare graves are a series of simple shallow graves rather than a family vault, with the graves of Anne and William the most shallow. Their burials are in shrouds rather than coffins, which may either be due to economics (coffined burials were more expensive) or to conserve space on the chancel steps for future family burials, since coffined burials took up more space.[48]

The chancel has often been thought of as a burial space which tithe holders like Shakespeare would have merited, but Robert Bearman points out that 'burial in the chancel can hardly be regarded as an honour or a right attached to an interest in the tithes but simply evidence of a willingness to pay the necessary fees'.[49] The reason Anne Shakespeare had a chancel burial in the 'most prestigious' part of the church is because her family was willing to pay a higher fee for a significant burial place.[50]

[46] Carrick Utsi and Colls, 'GPR Investigation', 349.

[47] Vanessa Harding, *The Dead and the Living in Paris and London, 1500–1670* (Cambridge: Cambridge University Press, 2002), 127–8.

[48] Carrick Utsi and Colls, 'GPR Investigation', 343, 351.

[49] Bearman, 'Ledger Stones', 6–7. Rodwell notes that those who could afford to 'buy their way into the church' often sought an indoor burial near the altar. *Archaeology of Churches*, 312.

[50] Justin Lovill, *Old Parish Life: A Guide for the Curious* (Cornwall: Bunbury Press, 2022), 347. The exact cost of a chancel burial in Holy Trinity Church is unclear. Henry Spelman complains that chancel burials elsewhere could run as high as £10 (*De Sepultura* [London, 1641], 26–28). See also Sherlock, *Monuments and Memory*, 178–9. The *Vestry Minute-Book* for Stratford in 1656 recorded: 'it was agreed and ordered that forasmuch as divers persons have neglected to pay for graves made in the church and will not pay without suites of law, that henceforth there shall noe grave be made in the church untill they shall first deposite the money therefore due, which is 6s. 8d. for every grave, into the hands of Richard Smyth, parrish clerke' (*The Vestry Minute-Book of the Parish of Stratford-on-Avon from 1617 to 1699*, ed. George Arbuthnot [London: Bedford Press, n.d], 80).

Following Anne's burial, the subsequent chancel burials for the Shakespeare family were Susanna Shakespeare Hall's husband John Hall (d.1635); Thomas Nash (d.1647), the first husband of Susanna and John Hall's daughter Elizabeth; and Susanna Shakespeare Hall (d.1649), though the ordering of the Shakespeare family graves on the chancel steps does not correspond to the chronological order of burial.[51] The absence of Judith Shakespeare Quiney from the chancel burial space has been the subject of much speculation, but Orlin persuasively argues that Judith 'may have been the keeper of the family flame' and that by 1662 no family members were left to memorialize her, over a dozen years after the death of her older sister.[52]

No will for Anne Shakespeare is known to have survived, but if Anne made a will, it may have clarified whether her chancel burial was planned by Shakespeare, was a result of her own request, or was initiated by her surviving family members.[53] One account, from 1693, seventy years after

---

[51] See Orlin, *Private Life*, 214–24. The order of the graves, from left to right is Anne Shakespeare, William Shakespeare, Thomas Nash, John Hall, and Susanna Shakespeare Hall. The placement of Thomas Nash's grave on the other side of Shakespeare's grave has puzzled historians. Bearman proposes that when John Hall died, a space was allocated for Susanna between her husband and her father, but Thomas Nash's death in 1647 disrupted that plan. The last lines of John Hall's epitaph (translated from Latin) state that 'his most faithful wife is here / And the companion of his life is now also with him in death', so Hall's gravestone could not have been completed until after Susanna's death in 1649. Bearman suggests that Nash's death in 1647 may have 'sparked off a new and more elaborate way of commemorating the family' which Nash may have left money to pay for, including a retrospective epitaph for John Hall done in connection with Susanna's grave (Robert Bearman, 'The Shakespeare Ledger Stones and What They Tell Us', in *Holy Trinity Church: A Taste of History*, ed. Ronnie Mulryne [Stratford: Stratford-upon-Avon Society, 2022], 37–38). Bearman also suggests that Elizabeth Barnard's second husband John Barnard may have paid to commemorate her family.

[52] Orlin, *Private Life*, 223. See also Laurie Maguire's forthcoming biography of Judith Shakespeare Quiney for more details about Judith's burial.

[53] Anne may have had a say in where she was buried. Barbara J. Harris points out that the location women chose for their tombs 'formed the foundation of the

Anne's death, and told by a clerk 'above 80 years old', relates that Shakespeare's 'wife and daughters did earnestly desire to be laid in the same grave with him'.[54] Could this 'desire' have been expressed in a will or other written document that no longer survives? However the Shakespeare family graves came about, their placement at the chancel would have been 'a striking reminder of power, continuity, and cohesion', a point that would have been reinforced as subsequent family members were buried alongside William and Anne Shakespeare.[55]

image they fashioned of themselves for posterity' (*English Aristocratic Women and the Fabric of Piety, 1450–1550* [Amsterdam: Amsterdam University Press, 2018], 123). It is worth pointing out that Shakespeare did not specify any burial wishes in his own will either, even though several other chancel burials in Holy Trinity Church were specified in wills. In his will of 1492/93, Dean Thomas Balsall requested that his body 'be buried in the chancel of the collegiate church of Stratford aforesaid in the monument of my ordering on the back side of the chancel'. John Combe, in his will of 28 January 1612/13, wanted his 'Body to be buried in the Parish Church of Stratford upon Avon . . . near to the Place where my mother was buried and my Will is that a convenient Tombe of the value of threescore pounds shall be by my Executors hereafter named out of my Goods and Chattels first raised within one year after my decease be sett over me'. Thomas Combe, in his will of 20 June 1656, recorded, 'my boodie I commit unto the earth from whence it was taken to be buried in the Channcell of the parish Church of old Stratford'. Thomas Rawlins in 1699 desired to be 'buried by my late wife and her Sons body in Stratford Chancell'. See Stephanie Appleton and Mairi Macdonald, *Stratford-upon-Avon Wills 1348–1701* (Stratford-upon-Avon: The Dugdale Society, 2020), 1:66, 307; 2:45. J. Roger Greenwood writes that 'the majority of known brasses have no matching will at all' ('Wills and Brasses: Some Conclusions from a Norfolk Study', in *Monumental Brasses as Art and History*, 83).

[54] John Dowdall, letter to Master Southwell, 10 April 1693 (V.a.74, Folger Shakespeare Library, transcribed in E. K. Chambers, *William Shakespeare: A Study of Facts and Problems* [Oxford: Clarendon Press, 1930], 2:259). See also Orlin, *Private Life*, 398–9.

[55] David Cressy, *Birth, Marriage, and Death: Ritual, Religion, and the Life-Cycle in Tudor and Stuart England* (Oxford: Oxford University Press, 1997), 463.

A prominent chancel burial like Anne Shakespeare's was desirable not only because of its proximity to sacred space, but also because it would be noticed by the clergy.[56] An epitaph from St Edmund's Church, Kingsbridge, Devon, for Robert Phillips (d. 1793), placed near the chancel door, underscores the distance of his grave to the altar:

> Here lie I at the chancel door;
> Here lie I because I'm poor;
> The farther in the more you'll pay,
> Here lie I as warm as they.

The location of a burial within the church demonstrated social status, and a premium location within the chancel testified to the importance of the deceased.[57] In Holy Trinity Church specifically, Robert Bearman explains that the 'desire for visual commemoration within the parish church had been taken up by affluent members of a rising middle class', such as the Shakespeare family.[58]

Not only would a prominent grave position secure perpetual visibility, the disruption involved in making the grave itself would also serve as a public announcement of a notable death. Most indoor burials consisted of shallow graves with slabs flush to the floor, like William and Anne Shakespeare's, but indoor burials were nevertheless messy and the 'constant upheaval of floors' would have created a floor that 'would have progressively degenerated into a patchwork of materials, forever sinking and uneven'.[59] Examples survive of complaints about unfinished or open graves in churches, including one in 1629 at All's Saints in King's Lynn, 'for breaking the pavement in the church for graves and not covering it

---

[56] Norris, *Monumental Brasses: The Craft*, 63. See also Julian Litten, *The English Way of Death: The Common Funeral since 1450* (London: Robert Hale, 1991), 200.

[57] Cressy, *Birth, Marriage and Death*, 461. [58] Bearman, 'Ledger Stones', 4.

[59] Rodwell, *Archaeology of Churches*, 313. Philip Schwyzer discusses burial practices in the works of Shakespeare in *Archaeologies of English Renaissance Literature* (Oxford: Oxford University Press, 2007), 108–50.

again'.[60] The usual process for affixing a brass like Anne's would have been to cut an indent in the stone slab to the exact size of the brass plate so that the plate would be level with the floor, and then attach the plate to the slab with a system of riveting which involved running molten lead underneath the brass plate to secure the rivets (visible in Figure 1). It is a process that would have been loud and disruptive, and best accomplished outside of the church.[61] In most cases, fixing a brass to a stone slab was carried out in the engraver's workshop, and delivery was part of the contract, but the expense 'restricted the practice to the wealthiest families'.[62] Stone slabs were sent 'in great quantity' to brass engravers in London (see Section 4).[63] These were likely the logistics involved in preparing Anne's grave. Suffice it to say, the installation of Anne's epitaph would have disrupted the community at Holy Trinity. Given the prominent position of her grave on the chancel steps, that part of the church would have been disturbed with the 'presence of

---

[60] Cressy, *Birth, Marriage, and Death*, 463.

[61] Bertram, *Monumental Brasses as Art and History* (Stroud: Allan Sutton, 1996), 21. See also Norris, *Monumental Brass: The Craft*, 33, 41. A record survives from St. John's, Canterbury, dated 1613 of a sum 'Payd for fast(en)ing the brass of the graves in the chaunsells' (R. H. D'Elboux, 'Testamentary Brasses', *The Antiquaries Journal* 29 [1949], 183–191). See also Sally Badham, *Monumental Brasses* (Oxford: Shire, 2009), 15. For his 1631 brass (by Edward Marshall), Archbishop Samuel Harsnett specified 'a Marble stone . . . with a Plate of Brasse moulten into the Stone an ynche thicke . . . the Brasse to be soe riveted & fastened cleane through the Stone as sacrilegious handes may not rend off the one without breakinge the other' (Nancy Briggs, 'Samuel Harsnett', *Monumental Brass Society Portfolio of Brasses* [November 2006], www.mbs-brasses.co.uk/index-of-brasses/samuel-harsnett).

[62] *Palimpsests* 1:100; Norris, *Monumental Brasses: The Craft*, 43. Norris notes that both the stone and the brass were transported by water where possible, though occasionally only the brass plate itself was sent. Cressy, *Birth, Marriage, and Death*, 463.

[63] Norris, *Monumental Brasses: The Craft*, 32–33, 88–98. See also G. Dru Drury, 'The Use of Purbeck Marble', *Dorset Natural History and Archaeological Society*, (1948), 74–98.

workmen's tools and open tombs', and the process and placement of her grave would have been apparent to her community.[64]

Anne was buried on 8 August 1623, and her brass epitaph was put into place at the latest by 1634, since it is recorded for the first time in a transcription of antiquarian William Dugdale's manuscript notes for July of that year.[65] Within this time frame, numerous community members who personally knew Anne (as well as family members) would have been alive to witness her burial and the subsequent installation of her epitaph. Epitaphs were often installed for an anniversary of the death of the commemorated person, along with a customary family gathering, which would make August of 1633 a likely end point.[66] While memorials were usually added within two years of death, it was not uncommon for a longer period to elapse between the date of death and the commemoration. Other works by the same engraver as Anne's epitaph (such as Katherine Gildredge, discussed in Section 4) had a gap of longer than a year between death and completion of a memorial. Furthermore, the end of the apprenticeship period for the engraver of Anne's epitaph makes a date from the late 1620s through 1633 a likely time frame.[67] It is possible that the brass plaque

---

[64] Cressy, *Birth, Marriage and Death*, 463.

[65] Tom Reedy, Private Correspondence. Dugdale's notes date his visit to Holy Trinity Church as 9 July 1634, but his notes also include inscriptions for John Hall, Susanna Hall, and Thomas Nash, so the page must be a later copy of the original notes (Reedy, 'William Dugdale on Shakespeare and His Monument', 194). Dugdale describes Anne's grave as 'a flat face stone with this inscription'. In the second edition of Dugdale's *Antiquities* in 1730, William Thomas described Anne's epitaph as 'on a brass plate in great [i.e. capital] Letters' (William Dugdale, *The Antiquities of Warwickshire*, augmented by William Thomas [London: John Osborn, 1730], ii: 685). George Vertue's drawing of 1737 describes it as a 'grave stone', and he reproduces a rectangular space for the epitaph, which according to Orlin is 'the brass plaque we now see for Anne Shakespeare'. *Private Life*, 215.

[66] Bertram, *Monumental Brasses*, 22.

[67] See Greenwood, 'Wills and Brasses', 95; Nigel Llewellyn, *Funeral Monuments in Post-Reformation England* (Cambridge: Cambridge University Press, 2000), 180; and Norris, *Monumental Brasses: The Craft*, 64–65. Gildredge died in 1629, and

replaced an incised slab, but there is no evidence to substantiate this, and it would not make sense for the family to pay for two forms of memorialization (both an incised slab and an engraved brass).

The Shakespeare family could have delayed installing Anne's epitaph until several years after her death for a variety of reasons.[68] It may have taken longer to secure an engraver of the calibre necessary to honour Anne (see Section 4). Although families usually maintained relationships with engravers, Nicholas Johnson, the sculptor of Shakespeare's monument, had retired by 1621 and died in 1624. No records survive to indicate who paid for Anne's brass plaque, but the financial difficulties of her daughter Susanna Hall and her husband John may have contributed to the delay. According to Orlin, as executors of Shakespeare's will, the Halls had to pay out 'the enormous amount of nearly £229 – well more than double what Shakespeare's properties brought in each year – within the space of twelve months'. The Halls had to sell Shakespeare's tithe rights, and Susanna's financial troubles continued even after the death of her husband.[69]

Another reason for the possible delay is that the chancel area of Holy Trinity Church was in a state of disrepair around the time of Anne's death in 1623. In 1618, the churchwardens complained that 'our chancel is ruinous and out of repayre', and the *Vestry Minute-Book* includes regular comments about money needed for church repairs.[70] The Shakespeare family may

her monument dates from 1635/36, since it includes the death of the date of her daughter Katherine in March 1635/36, most likely erected by their husband and father Nicholas Gildredge, who is also mentioned on the monument. John Lovekyn had a brass added to his tomb several years after his death. See Nigel Saul, 'What an Epitaph Can Tell Us: Recovering the World of John Lovekyn', *Ecclesiology Today* 43 (2010): 61–67.

[68] Orlin notes that John Hall's grave 'almost certainly stood bare for at least fourteen years' until Susanna's burial, which would have been a longer time than the delay with Anne's grave (*Private Life*, 221). The Shakespeare graves were backfilled at the time of burial so it is possible they remained in that state until ledger stones were available (Carrick Utsi and Colls, 'GPR Investigation', 349).

[69] Orlin, *Private Life*, 171.

[70] Paul Edmondson, 'The Church that Shakespeare Knew', in *Exploring Shakespeare's Church*, eds. Lindsay and Sandra MacDonald (Stratford-upon-

have wanted to wait until the chancel had been repaired, even if that took much longer than they may have anticipated. The chancel area was closed off from the rest of the church from 1618 until 1641, and the rood screen was placed across the chancel entrance until 1835.[71] As late as 1837, the chancel was described as having 'a broken, noxious and wet floor, with foundation walls gradually mouldering with the green damp from neglected drainage – timbers mildewing and rotting – limewashed walls – a flat plastered ceiling; and the whole presenting a scene of tasteless patchwork and miserable economy'.[72] Parish clerk Thomas Kite reports that, after the 1844 restoration, the Shakespeare graves were 'carefully covered with boards and a trap door constructed immediately over the Grave of Shakespeare which could be easily raised for visitors to see the Stone and read the Inscription'.[73] This of course would have made Anne's grave completely inaccessible in the later nineteenth century, so any visitors to the church would likely be unaware of the chancel graves other than Shakespeare's.

In addition to the disrepair of the chancel area of the church, the decade following Anne's death was a period of high tension in the town between zealous Puritan Thomas Wilson, who became vicar of Holy Trinity in May of 1619, and the more moderate Stratford Town Corporation. Wilson's 1619 arrival was heralded by a group of rioters outside the church, chanting that if they could 'catch the said Thomas Wilson, they would flay him and dispatch him of his life', as well as 'cut off his pocky and burnt member', and 'pull, drag, and haul him out of the church'.[74] Wilson's supporters locked him in the chancel for protection. His stipend was increased from £20 to £40 and then to £60 starting in 1623, and the churchwardens levied the parish

Avon: Independent Publishing Network, 2021), 85. See also Bearman, 'Ledger Stones', 79–100.

[71] See Orlin, *Private Life*, 219; Bearman, 'Ledger Stones', 6; Edmondson, 'The Church that Shakespeare Knew', 84.
[72] *Warwick Advertiser* (29 April 1837), cited in Macdonald, 'Not a Memorial to Shakespeare', 213.
[73] Bearman, 'Ledger Stones', 16.
[74] Ann Hughes, 'Religion and Society in Stratford upon Avon, 1619–1638', *Midland History* 19.1 (2013): 61–62.

large sums from 1619 until 1628, between £20 and £50 per year, for the repair of the church.[75] The Shakespeare family may have wanted to wait for a calmer time to commemorate Anne, and Ann Hughes notes that 'a more settled Stratford was emerging by the later 1620s'.[76] This may have been misguided, though, because in July of 1629 Wilson stopped preaching a weekday sermon and his stipend was reduced from £60 to £40. In the 1630s, Wilson was 'the main instigator of trouble', one who 'adopted a highly controversial ministerial stance', using the church as his 'personal stage' to denounce 'prominent and respected corporation figures' in his sermons.[77]

It is unclear what role Anne's son-in-law John Hall played in the creation of her epitaph, but his close relationship with vicar Thomas Wilson could have helped or hindered its progress, depending on Wilson's level of support.[78] Hall was a staunch supporter of Wilson throughout the period that Anne's memorial was created and put into place. In 1629, John Hall commissioned a carved pulpit for the church, and in 1633 he supported Wilson's case for an increase in salary.[79] In April of 1633 Hall was involved in a dispute about a pew Wilson had granted to John and Susanna Hall, and Thomas and Elizabeth Nash, 'for a kneeling place for hearinge divine service and Sermons'.[80] The placement of pews 'reflected the social hierarchy within the parish', and Hall went so far as to seek confirmation of his family pew

[75] Hughes, 'Religion and Society', 65. [76] Hughes, 'Religion and Society', 67.

[77] Hughes, 'Religion and Society', 71.

[78] Wilson was also connected to the Quiney family; Judith Shakespeare Quiney's brother-in-law George Quiney was Wilson's assistant minister (Macdonald, 'Not a Memorial to Shakespeare', 207).

[79] Orlin, *Private Life*, 220; and Ann Hughes, 'Building a Godly Town', in *The History of an English Borough: Stratford-upon-Avon 1196–1996*, ed. Robert Bearman (Stratford-upon-Avon: Sutton, 1997), 97–109.

[80] According to Bearman, 'John and Susanna Hall are granted the use of a seat "in the bodye" (probably the nave) of Holy Trinity Church, Stratford by a licence issued by John Thornborough, bishop of Worcester' (*Shakespeare Documented*, https://doi.org/10.37078/449). Christopher Marsh outlines the importance of pews in positioning parishioners according to rank and social order ('Order and Place in England, 1580–1640: The View from the Pew', *Journal of British Studies* 44 [2005]: 3–26).

from the Bishop of Worcester, John Thornborough, which he was awarded in 1635.[81] Hall joined the Corporation in 1632, perhaps to serve as an ally for Wilson, but this lasted barely over a year; he was expelled on 9 October 1633 'for wilful breach of orders, sundry other misdemeanours and continual disturbances'.[82] In June of 1635 Hall claimed he had paid for a new pulpit and that he and Thomas Nash contributed to repairs of the church.[83] Perhaps these repairs were related to an upcoming commemoration of Anne Shakespeare.

It is clear then that when William Dugdale visited Holy Trinity Church on 9 July 1634 (according to his manuscript notes) and transcribed the text on Anne's plaque, things were not exactly in order. By June of 1635, Wilson was suspended for a variety of offenses, including

> refusing to visit the sick, for walking in the Church during prayers, for holding Conventicles, for particularising some of his parishioners in his sermons, for profaning the chapel 'by sufferinge his children to playe at Bale and other sportes therein and his servauntes to hange clothes to drye in it, and his pigges and poultrie to lye and feed in it' and for sitting on the pulpit stairs to prevent his assistant, Mr. Trapp, from preaching a funeral sermon by request, the said Thomas Wilson being suspended for three months.[84]

---

[81] Hughes, 'Religion and Society', 74.

[82] Greg Wells makes this suggestion of John Hall as an ally in 'His Son-in-Law John Hall', in *The Shakespeare Circle*, 93.

[83] Orlin, *Private Life*, 400n38.

[84] Wheler papers (SCLA ER1/1/97, Shakespeare Birthplace Trust). See Hughes, 'Religion and Society', 69–70; and Diana Price, 'Reconsidering Shakespeare's Monument', *Review of English Studies* 48 (1997): 168–82. In *Shakespeare's Environment* (London: G. Bell and Sons, 1914), Charlotte Carmichael Stopes records repair of the chancel in March of 1691 by 'descendants of those who had monuments of their ancestors there', but 'there is no record of any descendants or friends of Shakespeare then' (118). See also Philip Styles, 'The Borough of Stratford upon Avon', in *Victoria County History of Warwickshire*, vol. 3 (London: Oxford University Press, 1946), 58, 269–276.

Still, Thomas Wilson and John Hall remained supportive of each other; when Hall died in November 1635, he was described in the burial register as '*medicus peritissimus* (a most skilled doctor)', likely a 'testimony to his local reputation' and to his 'close relationship' with Wilson.[85] At some point during Wilson's tenure, Anne Shakespeare's epitaph was installed, and given Anne's son-in-law John Hall's relationship to Wilson, the vicar likely was supportive of this commemoration. According to Charlotte Carmichael Stopes, Wilson probably officiated at Anne's funeral which would have included a sermon with a eulogy in her honour.[86] Among the many documents related to Anne Shakespeare that no longer survive, the absence of the text of the funeral eulogy that Wilson likely preached in honour of Anne, is particularly lamentable, as it would have offered additional insight into her character and reputation within her community. Similarly, since Anne's epitaph was likely in place within a decade of her death, the lack of surviving responses from local friends and neighbours who knew Anne personally is equally regrettable.

2 Materializing Memory: The Production of Anne Shakespeare's Epitaph

The material conditions involved in commemorating Anne Shakespeare tell the story of a woman whose survivors sought to memorialize her in the most permanent and meaningful way possible. As well as paying for a chancel burial, Anne's family devoted significant effort to preserving her legacy by creating an original Latin text for her epitaph and having it engraved on a commemorative brass plaque. The Halls had moved back into New Place after Shakespeare's death, which suggests a close-knit family who would have mourned Anne's death along with many others who knew her personally.

---

[85] Robert Bearman, 'Parish Register Entry Recording John Hall's Burial', *Shakespeare Documented*, https://doi.org/10.37078/464.

[86] Charlotte Carmichael Stopes, *Shakespeare's Warwickshire Contemporaries* (Stratford-upon-Avon: Shakespeare Head Press, 1907), 238. See also Cressy, *Birth, Marriage, and Death*, 408.

Around the time of Anne's death, early modern England experienced what Scott L. Newstok has called 'epitaphic saturation' and a 'preoccupation with this form of memorialization'. As the 'oldest of all genres', the epitaph was both a respected poetic form and a 'shorthand summatio[n]' of a life.[87] The seventeenth-century vogue for composing and collecting epitaphs is apparent from many popular printed histories, from William Camden's *Remains* (1605) to John Stow's *A Survey of London* (1598–1633) to John Weever's *Ancient Funeral Monuments* (1631).[88]

Epitaphs may have had particular significance to the Shakespeare family. Tradition has it that Shakespeare wrote his own epitaph, with its famous curse to prevent his remains from being moved to the nearby charnel house that occupied the north side of Holy Trinity Church until 1800.[89] Other epitaphs have been attributed to Shakespeare, most famously that of his friend John Combe, which Shakespeare was reported to have 'wright this att his request while hee was yett living'.[90] Shakespeare himself mentions epitaphs more frequently in his plays and poems than any other contemporary playwright.[91] The word 'epitaph' appears in his work seventeen times, often as evidence of sincere emotion, including Leonato's directive to

---

[87] Scott L. Newstok, *Quoting Death in Early Modern England: The Poetics of Epitaphs beyond the Tomb* (Basingstoke: Palgrave Macmillan, 2009), 8, 9, 13, 14.

[88] Claire Bryony Williams, 'Manuscript, Monument, Memory: The Circulation of Epitaphs in the Seventeenth Century', *Literature Compass* 11.8 (2014): 574. See also Dennis Kay, *Melodious Tears: The English Funeral Elegy from Spenser to Milton* (Oxford: Clarendon, 1990), 206–9 and 233–50, 573–582.

[89] The inscription reads: 'Good Friends, for Jesus' sake forbear, / To dig the bones enclosed here! / Blest be the man that spares these stones, / And curst be he that moves my bones'. See Bearman, 'Ledger Stones', 33.

[90] MS Ashmole 38, 180, Bodleian Library. Other epitaphs attributed to Shakespeare include one to Elias James (MS Rawl. Poet. 160, fol. 41, Bodleian Library).
A First Folio held by the Folger Shakespeare Library has three epitaphs written to Shakespeare in a seventeenth-century hand. See Heather Wolfe, 'Anonymous Manuscript Epitaph on Shakespeare, Written in a Contemporary Hand on the Rear Endleaf of a Copy of the First Folio', *Shakespeare Documented*, https://doi.org/10.37078/203.

[91] Newstok, *Quoting Death*, 165.

Claudio to 'Hang her an epitaph upon her tomb', Friar Francis's description of 'mournful epitaphs' hung 'on your family's old monument' (*Much Ado* 5.1 and 4.1), and Antonio's wish that Bassanio could 'live still and write mine epitaph' (*Merchant of Venice* 4.1). Epitaphs are also linked to memorialization for posterity, as Prince Hal refers to Hotspur being 'remember'd in thy epitaph' (*1 Henry IV* 5.4), Belarius warns of the danger of 'a slanderous epitaph' (*Cymbeline* 3.3), Hamlet notes the damage of a 'bad epitaph' (2.2), and Richard II declares, 'Let's talk of graves, of worms, and epitaphs' (3.2). Sonnet 81 even has an eerie resonance with Anne's epitaph, in its opening lines of one lover outlasting the other: 'Or I shall live your epitaph to make,/Or you survive when I in earth am rotten.' The speaker offers, 'your monument shall be my gentle verse' which shall outlast 'when all the breathers of this world are dead'.[92] When the Shakespeare family decided how best to memorialize Anne, the connotations of the epitaph as a sincere expression of emotion and a way to create an enduring legacy would have come to mind, as would the use of verse to immortalize a subject. However, as William N. West points out, even though there is a long history of the 'surprising durability of verse' dating back to ancient Greece, 'to name a poem as an enduring inscription does not make it so', and the choice of brass was as crucial to the survival of Anne's epitaph as was the verse itself.[93]

The selection of brass, as opposed to stone, as the material substrate for Anne's epitaph might have held particular significance for the Shakespeare family. Ben Jonson's verses 'To the Reader' in the 1623 First Folio, which appear on the page facing the Droeshout engraving of Shakespeare (Figure 5), were likely composed around the same time as Anne's death. There, Jonson refers to being 'writ in brasse' as the second-best way to immortalize his fellow poet, after the plays printed in the book. Shakespeare

---

[92] For an extended discussion of Shakespeare's sonnets and imagery of funeral monuments, see Simon Watney, 'Sky Aspiring Pyramids: Shakespeare and "Shakespearian" Epitaphs in Early Stuart England', *Church Monuments: The Journal of the Church Monuments Society* 20 (2005), Appendix 2 (115–6).

[93] William N. West, 'Less Well-Wrought Urns: Henry Vaughan and the Decay of the Poetic Monument', *ELH* 75.1 (2008): 198, 201.

Figure 5 Opening spread of Shakespeare's First Folio. Folger Shakespeare Library STC 22273 Fo.1 no.68

himself, in Sonnet 107, similarly posits poetry as the only 'monument' that endures longer than the strong material of 'tyrants' crests and tombs of brass'.

Shakespeare uses brass multiple times in his plays and poems to signify a lasting tribute, one that could outlast stone.[94] Henry V employs the image of graves with 'witness' that will 'live in brass' (4.3) as an inspirational legacy. Griffith in *Henry VIII* refers to 'Men's evil manners' which 'live in brass' (4.2), and Duke Vincentio in *Measure for Measure* describes 'characters of brass' which offer 'A forted residence 'gainst the tooth of time/

---

[94] See Lawrence Green, '"And Do Not Say 'tis Superstition"': Shakespeare, Memory, and the Iconography of Death', *Comparative Drama* 50 (2016): 249–70.

And razure of oblivion' (5.1). Richard II describes brass as 'impregnable' (3.2.), and Sonnet 64 refers to 'brass' as an 'eternal slave to mortal rage', a defence against decay and ruin. Titus Andronicus, when he commits to his course of revenge, calls for 'a leaf of brass' where 'with a gad of steel will [he] write these words' in order to preserve his legacy (4.1). The longevity of a poem 'writ in brasse' would not have escaped any reader of Shakespeare's works, including his family members.

In this context, the choice of brass instead of stone may signal the desire of the Shakespeare family to create a permanent monument to their matriarch, as both a testimony to her life and an inspiration for the future, a 'posthumous influence over the living'.[95] The main reason that Anne's epitaph has survived in relatively unspoiled condition is the fact that her family chose to commemorate her in the more durable form of brass as opposed to an incised slab, the more common form in the Midlands.[96] The graves of all the other Shakespeare family members buried at the chancel of Holy Trinity Church offer a case in point about the longevity of brass: their incised stone slabs had to be recut in 1844 because their lettering had become almost illegible.[97]

---

[95] Rory Loughnane, 'Afterword: Shakespeare and the Duties of the Living', in *The Shakespearean Death Arts: Hamlet among the Tombs*, eds. William E. Engel and Grant Williams (Cham: Palgrave Macmillan, 2022), 329. Humphrey Moseley uses a metaphor of brass to describe John Fletcher as a poet who 'never touched pen till all was to stand as firme and immutable as if ingraven in Brasse or Marble'. See Arthur F. Marotti, *Manuscript, Print, and the English Renaissance Lyric* (Ithaca: Cornell University Press, 1995), 261, 327–334.

[96] Norris, *Monumental Brasses: The Craft*, 46; J. G. and L. A. B. Waller, *A Series of Monumental Brasses from the Thirteenth to the Sixteenth Century* (London: John Bowyer Nichols and Sons, 1864), n.p. Charles Boutell observes that 'the durability of the brass plates' made them 'far more desirable than sculptured effigies' (*Monumental Brasses and Slabs: An Historical and Descriptive Notice of the Incised Monumental Memorials of the Middle Ages* [London: G. Bell, 1847], 4).

[97] There is no evidence that Anne's epitaph was ever recut. William Harness describes the restoration as a process of cutting stone, not engraving brass, by a 'man who is cutting the Shakespearian tombstones' (SCLA DR 125,

The fact that Anne's brass epitaph has survived intact further suggests that her grave was cared for by her survivors. Many of the brasses that survived the 1640s faced dereliction from 'dishonesty, carelessness, and apathy of the proper guardians of them', and some were even melted down to make church bells or chandeliers, or sold.[98] John Weever feared just such decay, and warned in his *Ancient Funerall Monuments* (1631) that inscriptions 'are broken downe, and utterly almost ruinated, their brasen Inscriptions erazed, torne away, and pilfered, by which inhumane, deformidable act, the honourable memory of many vertuous and noble persons deceased, is extinguished'.[99]

The use of brass as a commemorative material would have had additional significance for graves within Holy Trinity Church. Brasses were rare in Warwickshire; a total of just ninety-one brasses have been recorded, only thirty-seven of which date from 1600 to 1710.[100] Brasses were also rare at Holy Trinity at the time of Anne's death. Records survive for only three: one for Agnes Paget (d.1489), mistress of the Guild of the Holy Cross for eleven years; one for Frances Smith (d.1625) in the north aisle; and one or more (now lost) affixed to the tomb of Dean Thomas Balsall, who served as dean of the college and vicar of the church from 1466 to 1491 and was responsible for building the chancel in the 1480s.[101] The top of Balsall's

---

Shakespeare Birthplace Trust). Parish clerk Thomas Kite wrote in 1894 that the Shakespeare family graves' inscriptions were 'recut' in 1844, a practice for stone but not brass (Bearman, *Report*, 16). Ralph Lloyd-Jones remarks: 'Visiting Stratford upon Avon in 1844, Harness personally paid £3 to have Shakespeare's family monuments refurbished, including restoring the words "witty above her sex" to that of his daughter Susannah Hall' ('Harness, William (1790–1869), literary scholar', *Oxford Dictionary of National Biography*, 23 September 2004).

[98] Herbert Haines, *A Manual of Monumental Brasses: Comprising and Introduction to the Study of these Memorials*, Part I (Oxford: J.H. and Jas. Parker, 1861), cclvii–cclviii.

[99] John Weever, 'The Author to the Reader', in *Ancient Funerall Monuments* (London: Thomas Harper, 1631), n.p.

[100] Norris, *Monumental Brasses: The Craft*, 45.

[101] Bearman, 'Ledger Stones', 4. Dugdale mentions Agnes Paget's grave 'with a portraiture in brasse thereon' (*Antiquities of Warwickshire*, 518). The chancel at Holy Trinity would have had more engraved slabs than it does now, where the Shakespeare family graves are 'marooned in an entirely altered setting' (Bearman,

Figure 6 Anne Shakespeare's grave (bottom left) and the chest tomb of Dean Thomas Balsall (top left), Holy Trinity Church, Stratford-upon-Avon (author's own photo)

tomb still contains the indentations for the missing brasses, which no longer survive.[102] Anne's grave is next to Dean Balsall's chest tomb (see Figure 6), and the fact that both were commemorated with brass within steps of each

'Ledger Stones', 4, 15). See also J. Harvey Bloom, *Shakespeare's Church of the Holy Trinity of Stratford-upon-Avon* (London: T. Fisher Unwin, 1902).

[102] Bearman, 'Ledger Stones', 4. The tomb was damaged during the reign of Edward VI. See Edmondson, 'The Church that Shakespeare Knew', 82. In his 1656 *Antiquities of Warwickshire*, Dugdale records that 'The portraiture in brasse fixt on a great Marble stone, which covereth it, hath been long since torne away, as also the Inscription on the verge thereof' (517). See also Peter Marshall, *Beliefs and the Dead in Reformation England* (Oxford: Oxford University Press, 2002), 104–105, 174–179.

Anne Shakespeare's Epitaph 37

other would not have escaped notice by visitors to the church, and perhaps encouraged Anne's family to take special care to preserve her brass, given that Balsall's brass had likely disappeared by the time of Anne's death.

The exact cost of a memorial brass like Anne's is difficult to ascertain. The account book for Nicholas Stone (1586–1647) contains an entry for the memorial to Cecilia Puckering (c.1636) in St. Mary's Church, Warwickshire – a slab in the chancel floor with three brass plates of lesser quality than Anne's – which cost well over £10, including procuring, squaring, and smoothing the grave stone; obtaining the brass; cutting the inscriptions into the brass; riveting the brass to the stone; and gilding the brass letters.[103] Although Anne's grave would have been slightly cheaper with only one brass plate, £10 is still a significant cost, given that, in 1630, John Hall's possessions were only valued at £40 a year.[104] Paying to commemorate Anne in this way was not an insignificant expense.

---

[103] Walter Lewis Spiers, 'The Note-book and Account Book of Nicholas Stone', *The Volume of the Walpole Society* 7 (1918): iii–200, at 109. See also John Page-Phillips, *Macklin's Monumental Brasses* (London: George Allen and Unwin, 1978), 43n; and Norris, *Monumental Brasses: The Craft*, 32, 53–53. John Combe left £60 for his monument in Holy Trinity (Robert Bearman, *Shakespeare's Money* [Oxford: Oxford University Press, 2016], 172). Page-Phillips points out that while 'a brass could to some extent be made to suit a man's purse . . . the main part, the slab, with all its transport problems, was a considerable basic item of cost' (*Macklin's Monumental Brasses*, 37). In his will of 1604, Londoner Jacob Verzelini left £20 for marble stone with engravings of himself and his wife, along with 'some other remembrance or Epitaph' (D'Elboux, 'Testamentary Brasses', 190). D'Elboux estimates £1. 6s. 8d. for the 'normal price for a full-sized slab with a small-sized brass about 12 in, high, and inscription' ('Testamentary Brasses', 188).

[104] Bearman, *Shakespeare's Money*, 124. As a comparison, Eric Rasmussen estimates the 1623 Folio at 6*s*. 8*d*. per copy ('Publishing the First Folio', in *The Cambridge Companion to Shakespeare's First Folio*, ed. Emma Smith [Cambridge: Cambridge University Press, 2016], 18–29). Chris Laoutaris estimates that an unbound 1623 Folio would have cost 10s wholesale, and 15s unbound (*Shakespeare's Book*, 282). According to Stanley Wells, Shakespeare's

In addition to funding a chancel burial and a brass plate, Anne's family also would have provided the text of the epitaph, including the original Latin poetry, to the engraver in advance, as discussed in the next section.[105] Although no records remain for any of the Shakespeare graves, surviving documentation for other contemporary memorials suggests the process that would have occurred for Anne's commemoration.[106] The plan for a similar epitaph (Figure 7) for Thomas Herbert (d. 1681) survives in the British Library, where engraver Thomas Stanton was provided with the Latin text and layout for the epitaph, on a scale that resembles Anne Shakespeare's. Among the many other missing documents related to Anne Shakespeare, one especially laments the loss of the written manuscript text of Anne's epitaph with its potential traces of authorship.

A second set of records from Thomas Stanton, for the engraved slab for Jane Isham (d.1639), offers further evidence of the lost documents that would have once existed to plan Anne Shakespeare's epitaph. Figure 8 shows the Latin section along with the inscription 'Religiosa Deo, Casta Marito, Liberis Chara', ['Pious to God, Virtuous to her Husband, Dear to her Children']. Figure 9 contains the English portion, as well as the details about the engraver, 'Thomas Stanton by St. Andrews Church in Holborn Ston[e] Cutter' and the size of the slab, 'Ston[e] is to be 6 foote 9 inches long 2 foote & 9 inches broad'. Figure 10 shows the overall layout. Similar documents would have been produced as part of the planning process for Anne's epitaph, especially since the contents of the Latin portion of the epitaph were deeply personal and unique rather than deriving from a simple boilerplate text.

> monument in Holy Trinity cost between £20 and £30 ('A Close Family Connection: The Combes', in *The Shakespeare Circle*, 153).

[105] Llewellyn, *Funeral Monuments*, 179. Llewellyn points out that 'the information presented through iconography and lettering was much too important to be left to the choice of the tomb-makers and contracts specified that patrons had to supply details to supplement the tomb-makers' patterns and texts' (*Funeral Monuments*, 118).

[106] Adam White provides draft drawings for other period monuments in 'Funereal Monuments and Monumental Funerals: England in the Early Modern Period', in *Last Rites: Funerals and Funeral Monuments*, ed. Mark Kirby (London: Ecclesiological Society, 2024), 67–94.

Anne Shakespeare's Epitaph

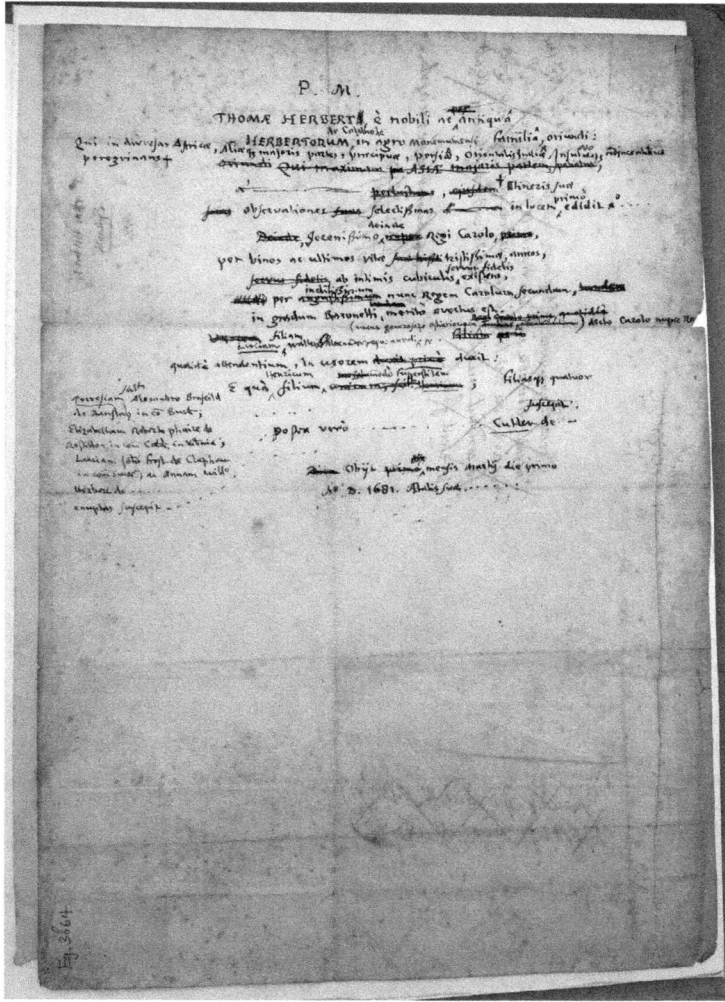

Figure 7 Plan for epitaph of Thomas Herbert (d.1681), St. Crux, York, by Thomas Stanton, British Library Eg 3864 627H

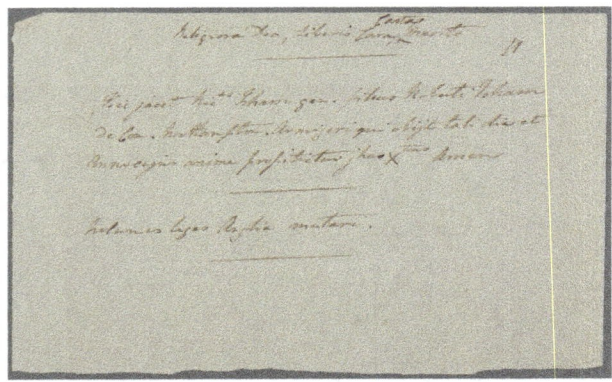

Figure 8 Plan for Jane Isham's engraving by Thomas Stanton, All Saints, Lamport, Northants, MS Northants, County Record Office IL 1635, Northamptonshire Archives

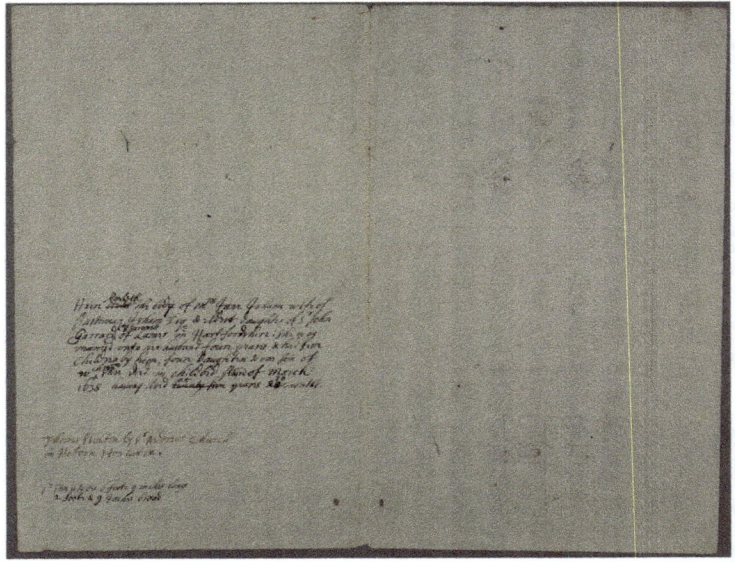

Figure 9 Plan for Jane Isham's engraving by Thomas Stanton, All Saints, Lamport, Northants, MS Northants, County Record Office IL 1635, Northamptonshire Archives

Anne Shakespeare's Epitaph 41

Figure 10 Plan for Jane Isham's engraving by Thomas Stanton, All Saints, Lamport, Northants, MS Northants, County Record Office IL 1635, Northamptonshire Archives

Even if lost archival documents resembling Figures 7–10 were to surface with details about who paid for Anne's epitaph along with the written epitaph in an identifiable hand, such texts still would still not provide definitive proof about authorship of the inscription, particularly the original Latin verses. The content of Anne's epitaph raises questions of authorship, and in the following section I will address both topics in tandem, laying out the likelihood of Anne's daughters as the 'authors' and originators of her epitaph. If we entertain the possibility that Susanna and Judith wrote Anne's epitaph it would be the only surviving 'Shakespearean' text written by women, and a significant testimony to her maternal role.[107]

---

[107] Matthew Steggle's attribution of the 'Spiritual Testament' to Shakespeare's sister Joan Shakespeare Hart is a potential additional example of literary activity by a woman from the broader Shakespeare family.

3 Memorializing the Maternal: Creating the Content of Anne Shakespeare's Epitaph

So far, I have argued that the material contexts surrounding the creation of Anne Shakespeare's epitaph – a costly chancel burial and a commemorative brass plaque – point to a more expensive tribute than was necessary, but one that was fitting for her important role in her family and in her community. The content of her epitaph is equally significant and extends far beyond the basic text on an early modern grave, which would have been a slab incised with birth and death dates.[108] The top section of the epitaph (Figure 11, cropped for effect), written in English and inscribed in Roman capitals, positions Anne as the wife of William Shakespeare: 'HEERE LYETH INTERRED THE BODY OF ANNE WIFE OF WILLIAM SHAKESPEARE, WHO DEP[AR]TED THIS LIFE THE 6TH DAY OF AUG[UST] 1623, BEING OF THE AGE OF 67 YEARES.'[109] This is a standard formula, replicated on countless brass plaques of the period, such as the examples pictured in Figures 12–14.[110]

'Here lyeth', the most common opening phrasing for an epitaph, has several layers of meaning.[111] 'Here' refers to the physical location of Anne's

---

[108] Several members of the Hathaway family had incised slabs in Holy Trinity Church, but not in a prime place on the chancel steps.

[109] To give just one of many examples, the brass to John Pen and his wife Sarah, attributed to Edward Marshall, has similar wording: 'Heere lyeth interred the body of John Pen of Pen Esquire who married Sarah the Daughter of Sir Henry Drury Knight by whom hee had issue five sonnes and five daughters hee departed this life the second of July A[nno]; D[omi]NI: 1641'. See Norris, *Monumental Brasses: The Craft*, plate 257.

[110] Llewellyn notes that 'most inscribed texts adopted some combination of discursive biography, epigram, poetry and motto' (*Funeral Monuments*, 127). Susan Broomhall points out that John Hall 'also visibly claimed his status as Shakespeare's legal inheritor on his 1635 funeral monument' ('"Let Me Weep for Such a Feeling Loss": The Emotional Significance of Shakespeare's Heritage', in *Historicising Heritage and Emotions*, ed. Alicia Marchant [New York: Routledge, 2019], 106, 99–113).

[111] For an extended discussion of the use of 'Here', see Newstok, *Quoting Death*, esp. 33–58; and Heather Dubrow, *Deixis in the Early Modern English Lyric: Unsettling Spatial Anchors like 'Here,' 'This,' 'Come'* (Basingstoke: Palgrave Macmillan, 2015).

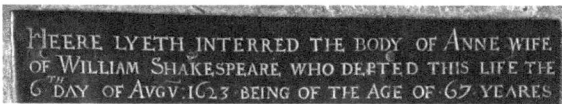

Figure 11 Anne Shakespeare's epitaph, Holy Trinity Church, Stratford-upon-Avon, cropped (author's own photo)

Figure 12 Epitaph of John Jener, All Saints Church, Laxfield, Suffolk, https://creativecommons.org/licenses/by/2.0/

Figure 13 Epitaph of Jane Osborne, Saint Withburga Church, Holkham, Norfolk, image courtesy of John Vigar

Figure 14 Epitaph of Humfrey Smith, Church of St. Peter, Farmington, Gloucestershire, image courtesy of Rex Harris

body, underneath the brass plaque. This was not the case for every burial, but recent archaeological work has verified that Anne's grave *is* actually underneath the stone with her brass plaque.[112] 'Here' also calls attention to the important location of her burial, nestled between Shakespeare's monument on the north wall, his grave, and chancel founder Dean Thomas Balsall's tomb.[113] 'Here' also highlights the location of the chancel steps, emphasizing the importance of a premiere burial space for Anne. The identification of Anne as 'wife of William Shakespeare' (the only place in the epitaph where Shakespeare is mentioned) establishes her family lineage and her relationship as his wife, in contrast to the sparse inscription on his grave, featuring only a curse but no name or other personal details.

The key bottom section (Figure 15, cropped for effect), in upper and lower script lettering in Latin – dismissed by Stephen Greenblatt as a 'strange inscription' and by Edmond Malone as 'not worth preserving' – is the most reliable and significant evidence that survives about Anne, well beyond the minimal section in English (Figure 11). The fact that this custom verse was composed and included on the plaque in the first place opens up new narratives about her role in the family.

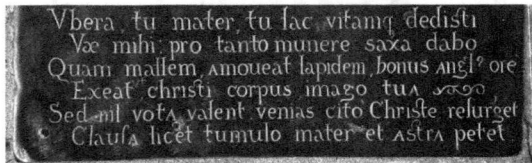

Figure 15 Anne Shakespeare's epitaph, Holy Trinity Church, Stratford-upon-Avon, cropped (author's own photo)

[112] See Carrick Utsi and Colls, 'GPR Investigation'.

[113] The placement of Anne's grave underlines Sarah Tarlow's point that 'at a death, emotional relationships were marked both in the form and wording of commemoration and in the location of the burial, as emotional proximity in life was extended and symbolically reproduced by spatial proximity in death' (*Ritual, Belief, and the Dead*, 109).

Anne Shakespeare's Epitaph

Vbera, tu mater, tu lac vitamque dedisti
    Væ mihi: pro tanto munere saxa dabo
Quam mallem, amoueat lapidem, bonus angelus orem
    Exeat, ^{vt} christi corpus, imago tua
Sed nil vota valent: venias citò Christe, resurget
    Clausa licet tumulo mater et astra petet.

You, Mother, gave [your] breasts, milk, and life;
Woe is me: in return for so great a gift I shall give rocks
How I'd prefer, I would pray, that the good angel should move the stone away
[And] out would come, like the body of Christ, the image of you!
But prayers are of no avail: come quickly, Christ, she shall rise again
[My] mother, although she has been shut in the tomb, and she shall seek the stars.

In line with contemporary practice, the Shakespeare family would have provided this text to the engraver when the commission for the brass plaque was set up, as noted in Section 2 and shown in Figures 7–10.

I suggest that the contents of the epitaph were deliberately designed to commemorate Anne as a mother, virtuous woman, and important member of her community.[114] It has sometimes been argued that since the Latin section of Anne's epitaph is written in a singular voice, it can only represent one of her daughters (Susanna), but the use of first person would have been standard for a commemorative poem of this type and does not necessarily

---

[114] Patricia Phillippy has described spaces of commemoration as 'sites for writing' and of 'special importance to women' in particular, where they could represent themselves ('"Monumental Circles" and Material Culture in Early Modern England', *Early Modern Women: An Interdisciplinary Journal* 4.1 [2009], 141), noting that 'contracts indicate that women patrons were responsible for delivering heraldic and visual details, as well as textual elements, to tomb sculptors' (146 n6), 139–147.

imply a singular authorship.[115] Thus, while Judith has rarely been credited with authorship, there seems no reason to omit her based on the use of first person.

Although Anne's epitaph is addressed from a child to a mother, it has most often been attributed to a man on Susanna and Judith's behalf, largely due to the need to be able to compose original Latin poetry. Susanna's husband John Hall has been the most common candidate. He was formally educated at Cambridge (BA and MA) and kept his medical records in Latin, and his own epitaph is also in Latin.[116] Another suggested author is Thomas Greene, who along with his wife Lettice lodged with the Shakespeares for at least eight years; Greene has been called 'the ablest man in town' next to Shakespeare and John Hall; and was also 'something of a poet who wrote Latin verses in his diary'.[117] Vicar Thomas Wilson had both the education and motivation to compose an epitaph for the mother of one of his most ardent supporters; he was said to be 'a very good Scholar, and was the son of a very grave conformable doctor of divinity'.[118] While it is certainly

---

[115] The variety of ways early modern women have been deemed 'authors' has been addressed by numerous studies, including Danielle Clarke's *The Politics of Early Modern Women's Writing* (London: Routledge, 2001), Laura Lunger Knoppers's edited volume *The Cambridge Companion to Early Modern Women's Writing* (Cambridge: Cambridge University Press, 2009), and Lara Dodds and Michelle M. Dowd, *Early Modern Women's Writing and the Future of Literary History* (Oxford: Oxford University Press, 2025).

[116] See Greg Wells, 'His Son-in-Law John Hall', 93. Greer attributes Anne's epitaph to John Hall 'ventroloquising for Susanna' (*Shakespeare's Wife*, 343). Weis contends that 'it is highly unlikely that either Susanna or Judith provided the Latin text, but instead may have been Judith's brother-in-law George Quiney' (*Shakespeare Revealed*, 370–1). Marlin E. Blaine's forthcoming work adds Stratford schoolmaster John Trapp as a possible but unlikely author.

[117] Edgar I. Fripp, *Shakespeare's Stratford* (Oxford: Oxford University Press, 1928), 59–60.

[118] Hughes, 'Religion and Society', 69. In addition to his close ties to John Hall in Stratford, Wilson also made periodic visits to London, specifically Blackfriars, where John Hall owned a house (Philip Tennant, *The Civil War in Stratford-upon-Avon* [Stroud: Allen Sutton, 1996], 1, 177n1). For

possible that one of these men translated Susanna and Judith's sentiments into Latin, several factors contribute to a strong case for the Shakespeare women as the authors.

First, the epitaph's striking originality implies that it was created specifically for Anne. Even after reading hundreds of epitaphs, I have yet to encounter one that resembles Anne's, and a search on EEBO-TCP for key phrases revealed no similar texts.[119] The epitaph derives from no traceable source nor is it a series of strung-together recognizable classical tags that one might expect from a commissioned local poet. Furthermore, the poem omits the conventional praises of female virtue and faith. In Victoria Moul's estimation, Anne's epitaph 'has certainly been written *for* her, either by or in consultation with her daughters'.[120]

The original content of Anne's epitaph is an especially crucial and reliable piece of evidence about her life because the conventions of epitaphic writing involved a degree of expected truth. Richard Brathwaite described epitaphs in 1619 as a way to 'manifest the sincerity of our loves, in erecting monuments over the dead, which might preserve their memory, and confirm our affections in their deaths'.[121] As John Bowden put it in his later work *The Epitaph-Writer* (1791), the 'chief Design of an Epitaph is to record and commend the Virtues of the Person on whose Tombstone it is written, and to excite the Reader to imitate them'.[122] As a literary form labelled as

a description of funeral customs and mourning protocols, see Cressy, *Birth, Marriage, and Death*, 379–474.

[119] The closest parallels are the seventh poem in George Herbert's sequence to his mother, Magdalen Danvers (1627) in *Memoriae Matris Sacrum*, which shares the Latin words *imago*, *ubera*, and *astra*, though the context and Latin verse are entirely different. Augustine's *Sermon 184* includes the line *Homo factus est hominis factor, vt sugeret vbera regens sidera*, 'The maker of man was made man, to suck at breasts while ruling the stars', a phrase often found in commonplace books and collections of quotations in the seventeenth century. Ben Jonson's poem to Shakespeare in the First Folio employs the 'seeking the stars' motif in its more typical mode. I am grateful to Victoria Moul for these references.

[120] Victoria Moul, personal communication.

[121] Richard Brathwaite, *Observations upon Epitaphs* (London, 1618), sig. D5v.

[122] John Bowden, *The Epitaph-Writer* (Chester: J. Fletcher, 1791), 52.

'the upholder of sincerity', an epitaph can often offer an especially accurate portrayal of the person commemorated.[123] The uniqueness of Anne's epitaph combined with the generic expectations of sincerity suggest that her daughters composed original poetry as a testament to their personal expressions of bereavement at her death, and that the epitaph is an exceptional expression of Anne's specific place in her family. In fact, the sentiments in the epitaph correspond to what G.W. Pigman describes as the second stage of mourning, a yearning that 'can last for months, sometimes years', where the 'bereaved behaves as if the dead could be recovered' and 'the bereaved intensely longs for and is preoccupied with the dead'.[124] Written from a child to a mother, Anne's epitaph is a profoundly personal tribute to her and a testimony of her daughters' grief. As Peter Ross puts it, the 'formality and finality' of commemorative conventions take 'all the mess of grief and loss and reduc[e] it to something that can be said with hammer and chisel'.[125] By looking at the contents of Anne's epitaph, we may be able to recover some details about her life that her daughters wanted to memorialize in this succinct format.

One obvious question is whether Susanna and Judith could have had the education possible to compose the original Latin verse. The Latin in Anne's epitaph is grammatically correct but syntactically awkward. The meter used, elegiac couplets, was the first type of verse taught to boys, and would not require extensive training to master. The lack of grammatical errors implies someone with reasonable experience of reading and writing Latin, but who may not read or write Latin verse on a regular basis. Based

---

[123] Scott Newstok, '"Here Lies": Sincerity and Insincerity in Early Modern Epitaphs on Stage', *Christianity and Literature* 67.1 (2017): 51, 50–68. See also Rachel Eisendrath, 'Object Lessons: Reification and Renaissance Epitaphic Poetry', in *The Insistence of Art: Aesthetic Philosophy after Early Modernity*, ed. Paul A. Kottman (New York: Fordham University Press, 2017), 59, 77–105.

[124] G. W. Pigman III, *Grief and English Renaissance Elegy* (Cambridge: Cambridge University Press, 1985), 7. Phillippy's descriptions of female mourning and lament resonate with the grief captured in Anne's epitaph. See *Women, Death and Literature in Post-Reformation England* (Cambridge: Cambridge University Press, 2002).

[125] Ross, *A Tomb with a View*, 93.

on these characteristics, the epitaph author(s) likely would have had at least a few years of grammar school or its home equivalent and that the quality of the Latin could be compatible with female authorship.[126]

No direct evidence survives of Susanna or Judith learning Latin or demonstrating their knowledge of Latin, but there are plenty of examples of early modern women attaining Latin literacy through education in the household, which was 'an important place of learning, teaching, reading, and copying', for both English and Latin texts.[127] Danielle Clarke concurs that most early modern women who were literate would have learned to read at home rather than in school. In the domestic space, women, most famously Queen Elizabeth I, even translated texts.[128] Surviving evidence from a 1598 deposition does indicate that there were opportunities for

---

[126] Ann Loftus offers a parallel example of a roughly contemporary woman writing in the 1640s who was capable of composing Latin verse, did not circulate in literary circles, and likely shared her Latin poetry only with family members. See Victoria Moul, 'Early Modern Women and Latin Literary Culture: Assessing the Evidence of Manuscript Verse', *English Literary Renaissance* 55.1 (2025): 1–34. Aemelia Lanyer and Rachel Speght also were fluent in Latin. Latin expert Oliver Nicholson offered a similar estimation, noting that the Latin is 'ingenious' but not 'elegant or inspired', and was probably written by someone who had the equivalent of a local grammar school education and learned Latin verse composition, but 'did not excel at it' (personal communication).

[127] Elizabeth Mazzola, *Learning and Literacy in Female Hands, 1520–1698* (London: Routledge, 2013), 3. Forthcoming work by Ailsa Grant Ferguson and Laurie Maguire will offer a reconsideration of both Susanna's and Judith's literacy. Evidence of early modern women's Latinity still remains woefully understudied. See Brenda M. Hosington, '"Minerva and the Muses": Women Writers of Latin in Renaissance England', *Humanistica Lovaniensia* 58 (2009): 3–43; Jane Stevenson, *Women Latin Poets: Language, Gender, and Authority, from Antiquity to the Eighteenth Century* (Oxford: Oxford University Press, 2005); and Victoria Moul, *A Literary History of Latin and English Poetry: Bilingual Verse Culture in Early Modern England* (Cambridge: Cambridge University Press, 2022) and 'Early Modern Women and Latin Literary Culture', 1–34.

[128] Danielle Clarke, 'Translation', in *The Cambridge Companion to Early Modern Women's Writing*, ed. Laura Lunger Knoppers (Cambridge: Cambridge University Press, 2009), 167–80.

female education in Stratford as early as 1575, and it is tempting to think that the Shakespeare women – Anne and her two daughters – may have attended the school.[129] According to one account, the number of women with a reading knowledge of Latin has been underestimated, based on the number of surviving Latin exercises by girls and Latin poems addressed to women.[130]

The Shakespeare women share many of the factors that Holt N. Parker has identified as increasing the likelihood of female Latinity, including being Protestant; and having a brother, a humanist father, or parents who 'believed in the moral value of *humanitas*'.[131] It is not unrealistic to imagine that Shakespeare's own daughters had extensive command of written language, perhaps extending to their ability to write an epitaph in Latin, along the lines of some of the women in Shakespeare's works who display various types of literacy.[132] Lady Macbeth is first depicted reading a letter from Macbeth, and while sleepwalking she will 'unlock her closet, take forth paper, fold it, write upon't, yet all this while in a most fast sleep' (5.1.3–7). Maria in *Twelfth Night* is an accomplished linguist who can read and write (and even mimic the handwriting of another); and Viola remarks that she has 'taken great pains to con' a speech that 'is excellently well penn'd' (1.5.153–55). Beatrice composes sonnets 'writ' by her own hand in *Much Ado About Nothing*, and Bianca in *The Taming of the Shrew* can translate Latin. Shakespeare's daughters may have learned Latin from him, since

---

[129] Jonathan Hope and Laura Wright, 'Female Education in Shakespeare's Stratford and Stratfordian Contacts in Shakespeare's London', *Notes & Queries* 43.2 (1996): 149–50. Marlin E. Blaine notes that 'educated Stratfordians read and wrote Latin not just in legal, religious, and epistolary texts but also in poetry'. 'Latin Culture in Early Modern Stratford', in *Book Culture in Shakespeare's Stratford: The Quiney Connections*, eds. Marlin E. Blaine, Lena Cowen Orlin, Alan H. Nelson, and Robert Bearman (London: Bloomsbury, 2026), 65.

[130] Moul, *A Literary History of Latin and English Poetry*, 4.

[131] Holt N. Parker, 'Women and Humanism: Nine Factors for The Woman Learning', *Viator* 35 (2004): 582–3.

[132] Mazzola, *Learning and Literacy*, 6. See Lisa Jardine's discussion of educated heroines in 'Cultural Confusion and Shakespeare's Learned Heroines: "These are old paradoxes"', *Shakespeare Quarterly* 38.1 (1987): 1–18.

some women were able to read and write verse in Latin and English 'simply because their fathers thought them educable'.[133] Hamnet Shakespeare offers another conduit for the possible education of Susanna and Judith, since girls were often educated alongside boys in a household.[134] The epitaph on Susanna's grave, describing her as 'witty above her sex', offers support for her learning, as does her 1639 signature, described by Rosalyn Sklar as 'clear and confident'.[135] A grave for Judith no longer survives to provide similar evidence, unfortunately.

Lost documentary evidence from New Place also has the potential to shed light on the literacy and literary activity of the Shakespeare women. In 1637, not long after Anne's epitaph was put in place, Baldwin Brooks, later bailiff of Stratford, broke into New Place. He did 'violently and forceablie to breake open the house in Stratford' and 'then and there breake open the Doores and studdy of the said howse, and Rashlye [did] seise upon and take Divers bookes boxes Deskes moneyes bonds bills and other goods of greate value as well w[hich] were of the said John Halls'. Susanna Hall and Thomas Nash attested that they did not know what was taken, since 'they had not then taken a full viewe survey or note of the personal estate of the said John Hall deceased'.[136] Even though the items are described as belonging to the 'personal estate of the said John Hall', the libraries of women were often 'incorporated into their husbands' holdings during their

---

[133] Jane Stevenson, 'Latin and Greek', in *The Oxford Handbook of Early Modern Women's Writing in English, 1540–1700* (Oxford: Oxford University Press, 2022), 63. See also MacKinnon, 'His daughter Susanna Hall', 74–76.

[134] Parker, 'Women and Humanism', 601. Jane Stevenson similarly notes that 'if a father decided to school his sons at home, which was not uncommon, it naturally increased the likelihood that daughters would learn Latin, since the children could be educated together', and fathers often taught their own daughters. 'Women's Education', in *Brill's Encyclopedia of the Neo-Latin World*, eds. Philip Ford, Jan Bloemendal, and Charles Fantazzi (Leiden: Brill, 2014), 95–96.

[135] Rosalyn Sklar, 'The Women Who Made Shakespeare: New Perspectives on the Female Relatives of William Shakespeare', *Women's History Today* 9 (2024): 31, 30.

[136] Transcribed in Frank Marcham, *William Shakespeare and His Daughter Susannah* (London: Grafton, 1931), 70.

lifetimes'.[137] The missing books, bonds, and bills could have been part of what William H. Sherman calls a 'matriarchive', where women used household printed books to 'store and circulate individual and collective records', including 'culinary, spiritual, familial, financial, intellectual, medical, and even meteorological information'.[138] These lost household papers may have contained the 'traces and absences' of texts attesting to the literacy of the Shakespeare women.[139]

The lost materials from New Place, especially the household papers, may have also offered links between female literacy and the experience of motherhood – a significant feature of the content in Anne's epitaph. Elizabeth Mazzola has argued that motherhood itself was a type of female literacy, involving 'retaining and reproduction of written knowledge' from mothers' advice books and motherhood stories.[140] Dorothy Clegge, for example, annotated a copy of William Gouge's *Of Domestical Duties* (1634) with her signature, a table of her family history, cross-references to Gouge's other works, and a list of her books.[141] If the Shakespeare women engaged in this type of textual practice at New Place, it is possible that books could have been incorporated into John Hall's library, confiscated in 1637, and to date, lost to history. The documents taken in this raid offer tantalizing possibilities.

The specific content of Anne's epitaph, particularly the Latin poetry, offers even more persuasive connections to the Shakespeare women and to female authorship. The boldly striking opening words of the Latin section, 'vbera' ('breast[s]') and 'mater' ('mother'), eulogize Anne as a breastfeeding

[137] Heidi Brayman Hackel, *Reading Material in Early Modern England* (Cambridge: Cambridge University Press, 2005), 214.

[138] William H. Sherman, 'Reading the Matriarchive', in *Used Books: Marking Readers in Renaissance England* (Philadelphia: University of Pennsylvania Press, 2008), 54, 59, 53–70.

[139] Susan Wiseman, 'Non-Elite Women and the Network, 1600–1700', in *The Oxford Handbook of Early Modern Women's Writing in English, 1540–1700*, eds. Danielle Clarke, Sarah C. E. Ross, and Elizabeth Scott-Baumann (Oxford: Oxford University Press, 2022).

[140] Mazzola, *Learning and Literacy*, 116–117.

[141] Sherman, 'Reading the Matriarchive', 61.

mother who gave 'milk and life', a tribute that would have signalled both Anne's achievements as a mother and her devoutness. The practice of breastfeeding was considered a 'testimony of love' and an example of the 'admirable work of God's providence', according to William Gouge in his 1622 *Of Domestical Duties*, which was reprinted at least a dozen times in the seventeenth century. John Dod and Robert Cleaver in *A Godly Form of Household Government* (1598; 1621) describe a good mother as one who 'nurse[d] her owne children'. Elizabeth Clinton in 1622 put it more bluntly: breastmilk comes from 'direct *providence* of God'.[142] As Marylynn Salmon remarks, 'a nursing mother represented selfless devotion to early modern men and women, for in feeding her child she gave, quite literally, of herself'.[143] Breastfeeding, Salmon notes, was 'a symbol for divine love' and 'represented God's gift of grace coming through his churches and ministers'.[144] Susanna and Judith's decision to foreground Anne as a breastfeeding mother was a way to underline her piety as well as the spiritual care and guidance that she provided for her family.

Further, breastfeeding was thought to evoke a stronger mother–child bond than wet-nursing. Gouge attested that 'together with the milk passeth some smacke of the affection and disposition of the mother: which maketh mothers to love such children best as they have given sucke onto; yea and oft times such children as have sucked their mothers breasts, love their mothers best'. Children who were wet-nursed, in contrast, would 'love

---

[142] William Gouge, *Of Domestical Duties* (1622), 509, 511; John Dod and Robert Cleaver, *A Godly Form of Household Government*, (London: R. Field, 1621), 95; Elizabeth Clinton, *The Countesse of Lincolnes Nurserie* (John Lichfield and James Short: Oxford, 1622), 10–11.

[143] Marylynn Salmon, 'The Cultural Significance of Breastfeeding and Infant Care in Early Modern England and America', *Journal of Social History* 28.2 (1994): 251, 247–269. See Olivia Langford's forthcoming University of Birmingham PhD dissertation, '"The raven doth not hatch a lark": The alien and maternal bodies of William Shakespeare's non-English mothers'; and David Harley, 'From Providence to Nature: The Moral Theology and Godly Practice of Maternal Breast-feeding in Stuart England', *Bulletin of the History of Medicine* 69 (1995): 198–223.

[144] Salmon, 'Cultural Significance of Breastfeeding', 252–3.

those nurses all the days of their life', even though, as wet-nursing advocates pointed out, the mother's fertility increased when she did not breastfeed.[145] Laura Gowing has argued that breastfeeding was 'emblematic of virtuous maternity' which was 'the ultimate feminine role'.[146] The reference to Anne as a breastfeeding mother thus served as a shorthand to characterize her as a virtuous and dutiful mother and, in the words of one historian, 'the epitome of the good mother'.[147] Both Susanna and Judith were mothers at the time of Anne's death, and their elevation of motherhood in Latin poetry on the chancel steps of their parish church and in brass would surely have been personally significant.

Commemorating Anne as a breastfeeding mother was also a way to call attention to her maternal moral heritage, since it was believed that 'a mother's virtuous character is transmitted to her children through her breast milk.'[148] Numerous scholars have argued that breastfeeding, as a 'spiritual vocation' of 'beloved duty and dutiful love', was both 'a sign of a mother's selflessness and sacrifice' and, in its empowerment of women, a 'potential disruption of patriarchal order'.[149] Donna C. Woodford points out that due to the belief that a child received spiritual nourishment from nursing, the practice gave the nursing mother or wet-nurse 'a tremendous power over

---

[145] William Gouge, *Of Domestical Duties* (1622), 512. See also Valerie Fildes, *Wet-Nursing: A History from Antiquity to the Present* (Oxford: Oxford University Press, 1988).

[146] Laura Gowing, *Common Bodies: Women, Touch and Power in Seventeenth-Century England* (New Haven: Yale University Press, 2003), 198.

[147] Harley, 'From Providence to Nature', 221.

[148] Femke Molekamp, *Women and the Bible in Early Modern England: Religious Reading and Writing* (Oxford: Oxford University Press, 2013), 107.

[149] Joanna Wolfarth, *Milk: An Intimate History of Breastfeeding* (London: Weidenfeld & Nicolson, 2023), 23; Rachel Trubowitz, '"But Blood Whitened": Nursing Mothers and Others in Early Modern Britain', in *Maternal Measures: Figuring Caregiving in the Early Modern Period*, eds. Naomi J. Miller and Naomi Yavneh (Aldershot: Ashgate, 2000), 85, 1-25; Naomi J. Miller, 'Mothering Others: Caregiving as Spectrum and Spectacle in the Early Modern Period', in *Maternal Measures*, 5.

the shaping of the child'.[150] It is hard to imagine a male author like John Hall or Thomas Wilson eulogizing Anne with the unique references to breastfeeding and maternal virtue, without the influence or direction of Susanna and Judith.

In addition to using breastfeeding as a way to exemplify Anne's power as a mother, the epitaph also contains multiple Biblical resonances. The theme of giving recurs, with 'gave' twice in the first two lines ('dedisti' and 'dabo'), and the description of Anne as 'so great a gift' ('pro tanto munere') echoes Ephesians 4:7 ('But unto every one of us is given grace, according to the measure, of the gift of Christ') and Romans 6:23 ('For the wages of sin is death; but the gift of God is eternal life, through Jesus Christ our Lord').[151] Lines 2–3 of the Latin section also recall verses from Matthew 7:9 ('Or what man is there of you, whom if his son asks for bread, will he give him a stone?'), Matthew 28:2 ('And behold, there was a great earthquake; for an angel of the Lord descended from heaven, and came and rolled away the stone, and sat upon it'), and Mark 16:3 ('And they asked each other, "Who will roll the one away from the entrance of the tomb?"'). Even though the epitaph has no direct source, it contains several biblical echoes that align Anne's personal qualities with a Christian tradition of charity, giving, and resurrection.

The last four lines of the Latin verse offer a more direct comparison between Anne and the central Christian image of resurrection, even comparing her 'form' ('imago', which could also be translated as 'spirit' or 'likeness') to the body of Christ ('Christi corpus').[152] The specific placement of Anne Shakespeare's grave, between the grave and monument of her husband and the tomb of Dean Thomas Balsall (see Figure 6), provides another context for the resurrection image in the epitaph. In addition to the

[150] Donna C. Woodford, 'Nursing and Influence in *Pandosto* and *The Winter's Tale*', in *Performing Maternity in Early Modern England*, 183–195.

[151] Marlin E. Blaine has pointed out to me that 'pro tanto munere' also directly echoes pseudo-Seneca's *Octavia*, and 'vota valent' echoes Martial and Ovid. See 'Latin Culture'.

[152] For other epitaphs that alluded to the resurrection, see Marshall, *Beliefs and the Dead*, 200–202, 229.

connection between Anne's brass and the brasses that once existed on top of Balsall's tomb, Balsall's memorial was designed as an Easter Sepulchre and originally featured scenes from the Passion (damaged in the sixteenth century), including one of the Entombment and one of the Resurrection.[153] Balsall was also commemorated in a window inscription, 'Thomas Balshall, Doctor of Divinity, reedifyed this quier and dyed anno 1491', recorded by Dugdale in 1656, which the Shakespeare family certainly would have known.[154] Remains of medieval stained glass in Holy Trinity depicting the Resurrection and Ascension may also have resonated with the content of Anne's epitaph.[155] Balsall's tomb had been in place since his death in 1491 and would have been a central feature for any visitor to Holy Trinity Church, including the Shakespeare family. Along with the missing brass inlays on top of Balsall's tomb that could have called to mind Anne's brass epitaph, so too would the Resurrection imagery in Anne's epitaph and the carving of the same scene mere feet away. Like the misericords in Holy Trinity (also from Balsall's time) that have been suggested as an influence on Shakespeare's work, so too would Balsall's tomb iconography have affected how Anne Shakespeare was memorialized, with the Resurrection imagery in her epitaph connecting her to an important church figure.[156]

It is also possible that Anne herself had a hand in how she was immortalized. Lady Jane Cornwallis Bacon (d.1659) planned her own monument with sculptor Thomas Stanton, and other contemporaries composed their

---

[153] 'The borough of Stratford-upon-Avon: Churches and charities', in *A History of the County of Warwick: Volume 3, Barlichway Hundred*, ed. Philip Styles (London: Oxford University Press, 1945), 275, 221-282. Balsall's elaborate memorial originally would have been covered with white lead and then painted, featuring scenes from the passion and resurrection replete with gilding (David Odgers, 'Conservation of the Chancel Monuments', in Mulryne, *Holy Trinity Church*, 22).

[154] Dugdale, *The Antiquities of Warwickshire*, 517.

[155] Edmondson, 'The Church that Shakespeare Knew', 86.

[156] On the misericords, see e.g. M. Lindsay Kaplan, 'Who Drew the Jew that Shakespeare Knew? Misericords and Medieval Jews in *The Merchant of Venice*', *Shakespeare Survey* 66 (2013): 298–315.

own epitaphs or gave directions for the contents of a brass engraving.[157] Elizabeth Cooke Hoby Russell also wrote several funerary inscriptions for her male relatives, including neo-Latin elegies and epitaphs.[158] Within Holy Trinity, Joyce Clopton also had a hand in her own commemoration, and in the memorial to her waiting gentlewoman Amy Smith (d. 1626). Although no will or other personal papers directly connected to Anne Shakespeare survive, it is doubtful that she would have disagreed with this celebration of her achievements as a pious mother, in the liturgical heart of the church.[159]

---

[157] *The Private Correspondence of Jane Lady Cornwallis Bacon, 1613–1644*, ed. Joanna Moody (Madison: Fairleigh Dickinson University Press, 2003), 47 n69; and Llewellyn, *Funeral Monuments*, 119–20. George Munnes requested 'a fair marble stone with my name graven in brass with the day and year wherein I shall be buried shall be fixed in the same', and John Coggeshall wanted 'a convenient marble stone upon my grave for the covering thereof' as well as 'some superscription in brass' or 'else some inscription of brass upon the church wall near unto my said grave, with my whole arms and scutcheon in the same to be graven' (Orlin, *Private Life*, 215). Barbara J. Harris writes that women's commemorative practices provided 'an opportunity to proclaim and memorialize the identities by which they wanted to be remembered' (*English Aristocratic Women and the Fabric of Piety, 1450–1550*, 119). Peter Sherlock offers numerous examples of women who 'publicly expressed their identity and sought to shape how they would be remembered through the authorship of epitaphs and the patronage of monuments' ('Monuments and Memory', 292). This also supports Patricia Phillippy's argument that early modern commemorative spaces provided 'a unique venue for women's writing and a means for women to forge and preserve female alliances, both within families and beyond' ('Monumental Circles', 145).

[158] See Jaime Goodrich, 'Class, Humanism, and Neo-Latin Epitaphs in Early Modern England: The Funerary Inscriptions of Elizabeth Cooke Hoby Russell', *Sixteenth-Century Journal* 49.2 (2018): 339–68.

[159] Nigel Llewellyn observes that 'mothering was a woman's most important role and an aspect of female experience referred to constantly on monuments', and that commemorating a mother 'confirmed a woman's social status' (*Funeral Monuments*, 287). See also Angus McLaren, *Reproductive Rituals*, 32, 60. If Anne's will survived, it may have had instructions for her burial, such as those for one John Smart of Plumstead who wanted to be buried in the church porch

If Susanna and Judith were indeed responsible for the composition of Anne's epitaph, then the choice of Latin would also have been theirs. The decision to eulogize Anne in Latin rather than in English raises many questions, especially since Latin would have restricted the ability of many to read the content. George Puttenham described the function of epitaphs in 1589 as designed 'for the passerby to peruse and judge upon', but this presumes that they can read the epitaph in the first place.[160] Although few readers in this period would have been able to read Latin, it would have been a way to further validate motherhood as worthy of commemoration on the chancel steps and to craft a more permanent memorial.[161] William N. West has observed that writing in Latin or Greek, as opposed to English, signalled a desire to evoke a more lasting work, and Margaret W. Ferguson points out that Latin had 'considerable cultural capital'.[162] Latin 'connoted learning' and would only be decipherable to 'literate observers', which had been the case persistently until 2023 when an

'with a stone the price xiijs iiijd with a certain remembrance in writing upon it in Laten testifying who lyeth there, praying, for my soule' (D'Elboux, 'Testamentary Brasses', 187). Andrea Brady points out that 'no account of funeral expenses has yet been found to include payment for elegiac composition' (*English Funerary Elegy in the Seventeenth Century: Laws in Mourning* [Basingstoke: Palgrave, 2006], 25). Newstok offers a few rare examples of wills that include directions for epitaphs, including one from 1622, though he notes that the practice was 'still comparatively uncommon' (*Quoting Death*, 21).

[160] George Puttenham, *'The Arte of English Poesie' by George Puttenham: A Critical Edition*, eds. Frank Whigham and Wayne A. Rebhorn (Ithaca: Cornell University Press, 2007), 144.

[161] Llewellyn, *Funeral Monuments*, 120, 123. John Donne's Latin prose epitaph written for his wife Anne in 1617 employed 'the language of law, theology, the Church and the ecclesiastical courts, [which] lent an air of *gravitas* and authority' to the epitaph. Bryan Rivers, 'Raeminae Lectissimae Dilectissimaeque': John Donne's Epitaph on his Wife, and the Elizabethan *Homily of the State of Matrimony*', *Notes and Queries* 59.1 (2012): 94–96.

[162] West, 'Less Well-Wrought Urns', 203; and Margaret W. Ferguson, *Dido's Daughters: Literacy, Gender, and Empire in Early Modern England and France* (Chicago: University of Chicago Press, 2003), 9, 16.

English translation was made available.[163] Commemorating Anne as a mother in Latin, a language with 'a far greater prestige in this period than any vernacular, let alone English', points to Susanna and Judith's clear intent to elevate the concept of maternity, even if it meant fewer people could read the inscription.[164] The opportunity to create a written testimony to both motherhood and to their personal grief may have even offered 'a means of authorizing and empowering women's speech', as Patricia Phillippy describes it.[165] Perhaps Susanna and Judith were playfully invoking the phrase on their father's monument, to 'read if thou canst' (as well as the Latin on his monument) while making an implicit argument about their own linguistic abilities and about the value of motherhood.[166]

Remarkably, the original Latin section makes no reference to Shakespeare, nor does it describe Anne as a wife. In the poetry likely composed fully or in part by her daughters, Anne is free of the longstanding focus on Shakespeare that has conditioned most of her afterlife and instead is honoured for her own accomplishments as a life-giving mother and a pious woman. Echoing Gail Kern Paster's view that narratives about birth and nurture are inscribed 'within and about the available discourses of power', Anne's epitaph exemplifies the potential power of the female maternal body.[167] In fact, Adrian Wilson argues that 'the ceremony of childbirth represented a successful form of women's *resistance* to masculine authority and power'.[168] By focusing on motherhood as

[163] Llewellyn, *Funeral Monuments*, 124.
[164] J. W. Binns, *Intellectual Culture in Elizabethan and Jacobean England: The Latin Writings of the Age* (Wiltshire: Redwood Press, 1990), 2–3.
[165] Phillippy, *Women, Death and Literature*, 3; and *Shaping Remembrance from Shakespeare to Milton* (Cambridge: Cambridge University Press, 2018), 14.
[166] The practice of writing epitaphs was 'an honourable act of memory, a tribute to the dead and a display of one's own skill' (Peter Sherlock, 'Monuments and Memory', in *A History of Early Modern Women's Writing*, ed. Patricia Phillippy [Cambridge: Cambridge University Press, 2018], 206, 292-312).
[167] Gail Kern Paster, *The Body Embarrassed: Drama and the Disciplines of Shame in Early Modern England* (Ithaca: Cornell University Press, 1993), 165.
[168] Adrian Wilson, *Ritual and Conflict: The Social Relations of Childbirth in Early Modern England* (London: Routledge, 2013), 196, emphasis in the original.

worthy of commemoration, Anne's daughters also engaged in a potentially subversive act by highlighting 'what qualities society should value and accordingly preserve in its collective memory'.[169] The epitaph is thus a remarkable testament to the life-giving and nurturing maternal body, positioned between the tomb of a pivotal church father (Dean Thomas Balsall) and the grave and monument of Stratford's most famous literary and biological father (William Shakespeare).

Attributing Anne's epitaph to her daughters Susanna and Judith has several implications. As the surviving women of the family, Susanna and Judith would have taken part in the physical preparation of Anne's body for burial. Her funeral would have been followed by a meal for mourners at her home of New Place, a further reminder of her position within her community and of the familial loss. As Gail Horst-Warhaft puts it, the traditional mourning process gave women 'potential authority over the rites of death', and Susanna and Judith's oversight of their mother's funeral preparations could have extended to authoring her epitaph.[170] After all, brass epitaphs were designed both to memorialize 'the character and achievements of the commemorated', and to 'stimulate the thought of the passer-by' and 'aid in the contemplation and discipline of the commemorated',[171] underlining the sentiment that 'personal relationships do not cease at death'.[172] The

[169] Joshua Scodel, *The English Poetic Epitaph: Commemoration and Conflict from Jonson to Wordsworth* (Ithaca: Cornell University Press, 1991), 140.

[170] Gail Horst-Warhaft, *Dangerous Voices: Women's Laments and Greek Literature* (New York: Routledge, 1992), 99.

[171] Lauren Cantos, 'Maternal Breastfeeding: Providence and Advocacy in Seventeenth-Century Sermons and Prescriptive Literature', in *Religion and Life Cycles in Early Modern England*, eds. Caroline Bowden, Emily Vine, and Tessa Whitehouse (Manchester: Manchester University Press, 2021), 71, 65–87; Norris, *Memorial Brasses: The Craft*, 61, 64. Bryan Rivers remarks that 'epitaphs eulogise the dead, but are written for the living'. '"Raeminae Lectissimae Dilectissimaeque": John Donne's Epitaph on his Wife, and the Elizabethan *Homily of the State of Matrimony*', *Notes and Queries* 59.1 (2012): 94.

[172] Tarlow, *Ritual, Belief and the Dead*, 10. Emily Shortslef observes that epitaphs show the 'capacity uniquely to represent the dead and maintain their connection to the living' and could 'generate a powerful sense of the personalities of those

Shakespeare family women may have taken inspiration from Anne's epitaph: Susanna when she buried her husband John Hall in 1635; Judith when she buried both of her other two sons – 19-year old Thomas and 21-year-old Richard – in 1639; and Elizabeth when she buried her first husband Thomas Nash in 1647, her own mother two years later. It is likely that we will never know for certain if Susanna and Judith were the ones who actually put pen to paper and composed the Latin verses on their own, or if they were part of the 'rich culture of Latinity' among early modern women, but the choices informing the text of Anne's epitaph – eulogizing her as a beloved mother in Latin and in brass – reflect the relationship between mother and daughters and thus belong to Susanna and Judith.[173] It remains a remarkable feat that Anne's daughters (who were themselves mothers) were invested in preserving her image as a mother, rather than as Shakespeare's wife. Though the 'real' Anne Shakespeare remains elusive, the 'Anne' preserved on her epitaph likely offers the truest version we can now access, given the conventions of epitaph writing and the epitaph's proximity to her death.

4 Beyond the Words: The Engraver of Anne Shakespeare's Epitaph

In the last section of this Element, I make a case that the creator of Anne's epitaph was a London-based engraver, whose networks offer further possible connections between Anne and the London literary

---

whom they continue to commemorate'. 'Acting as an Epitaph: Performing Commemoration in the Shakespearean History Play', in *Shakespeare and Commemoration*, eds. Clara Calvo and Ton Hoenselaars (New York: Berghahn Books, 2019), 14, 110. Another monument by the same engraver as Anne's (see Section 5), to Elizabeth Culpeper (1582–1638) in All Saints, Holingbourne, includes an inscription referring to her as 'Optima Faemina, Optima Coniux, Optima Mater,' 'the best of women, the best of wives, the best of mothers' (C. B. Newham, *Country Church Monuments* [London: Particular Books, 2022], 465).

[173] Diana Robin, 'Gender', in *The Oxford Handbook of Neo-Latin*, eds. Sarah Knight and Stefan Tilg (Oxford: Oxford University Press, 2015), 373.

world and thus expand her potential reach beyond the local confines of Stratford-upon-Avon. London workshops dominated the production of brass until the middle of the seventeenth century, 'turn[ing] out enormous numbers of brasses consisting simply of a small rectangular inscription plate laid across the middle of the stone' exactly like Anne's.[174] Most London-made brasses were also set into stone in the workshop. Herbert Druitt observes that London engravers 'supplied the greater number of brasses', because 'provincial engravers, as a rule, show inferior workmanship'.[175] According to contemporary practice, a brass epitaph like Anne's would probably have been produced in London rather than locally in Warwickshire. As part of their desire to memorialize Anne in a significant and important format, her family enlisted a top-notch engraver rather than someone who was local (and presumably second-rate). In what follows, I set out the case for the prominent London sculptor Edward Marshall as the likely engraver of Anne's epitaph, suggest several scenarios for how this commemoration of Anne could have come about, and underscore the implications of this new discovery, which offers tantalizing links between Anne and the printing and literary world of London.

Edward Marshall (1597/8–1675) was a distinguished London sculptor and mason with a long career, spanning the 1620s through the 1660s. He has been described as 'one of the best known sculptors of his time' and was on friendly terms with many literary figures, including Michael Drayton, John Aubrey, Francis Quarles, Ben Jonson, and John Smethwick, the latter a member of the syndicate of publishers who financed the printing of the

---

[174] Bertram, *Monumental Brasses as Art and History*, 14. See also Norris, *Monumental Brasses: The Craft*, 46, 81. Henry Wallis's painting 'A Sculptor's Workshop, Stratford-upon-Avon, 1617,' exhibited at the Royal Academy in 1857, depicts a fictional scene of Gerard Johnson carving Shakespeare's monument, with Ben Jonson holding Shakespeare's death mask. No sculptor had a workshop in Stratford-upon-Avon, especially with a view of Holy Trinity Church.

[175] Herbert Druitt, *A Manual of Costume as Illustrated by Monumental Brasses* (London: Alexander Moring, 1906), 12–13. See also Haines, *A Manual of Monumental Brasses*, ccxiv.

First Folio.[176] In addition to creating church monuments, monumental brasses, and masonry, Marshall was appointed Master Mason to the Crown from 1660 until his death in 1675 and was involved in rebuilding houses destroyed in the Great Fire of 1666. His various projects included the portico at The Vyne, Hampshire in 1654; Northumberland House in the Strand, London (1655–57); and Gunnersbury House in Middlesex (1658), as well as monuments to Michael Drayton, Inigo Jones, and the Earl of Totnes, among many others. His workshop sent monuments as far as Yorkshire.[177] Marshall had a prosperous and successful career; in 1662 he was assessed for 12 hearths, when the average property in nearby Fleet Street had 7.5 hearths.[178]

Sometime around 1629 Marshall moved from the parish of St. Martin in the Fields, Westminster, to the parish of St Dunstan in the West, and then to Pink's Alley near Fetter Lane.[179] In the parish rate books for 1628–29, he

---

[176] Katharine A. Esdaile, *Temple Church Monuments* (London: George Barber, 1933), 79; and Katharine A. Esdaile, 'The Gunpowder Plot in Needlework', *Country Life* (18 June 1943): 1094.

[177] Adam White, 'Marshall, Edward (1597/8–1675), Sculptor and Master Mason', *Oxford Dictionary of National Biography*. 23 September 2004, www-oxforddnb-com.ezp1.lib.umn.edu/view/10.1093/ref:odnb/9780198614128.001.0001/odnb-9780198614128-e-18133. See also Douglas Knoop and G. P. Jones, *The London Mason in the Seventeenth Century* (Manchester: Manchester University Press, 1935), 34; and Allison E. Sharpe, 'A Paget Memorial in Perspective: Aspects of a Seventeenth-Century Funerary Monument Erected to Richard Paget in St Mary's, Skirpenbeck, East Riding of Yorkshire', *The Antiquaries Journal* 70.1 (1990): 69, 65–81.

[178] Andrew Wareham, 'The Hearth Tax and Empty Properties in London on the eve of the Great Fire', *The Local Historian* 41 (2011): 284, 278–292.

[179] The best sources for Edward Marshall are Adam White, 'A Biographical Dictionary of London Tomb Sculptors, c.1560–c.1660', *Volume of the Walpole Society* 61 (1999): 83–94; and ' A Biographical Dictionary of London Tomb Sculptors, c. 1560–1660: Addenda and Corrigenda', *Volume of the Walpole Society* 71 (2009): 325–55, which I have relied on for this section. See also the entry on Marshall in Ingrid Roscoe, *A Biographical Dictionary of Sculptors in Britain, 1660–1851* (New Haven: Yale University Press, 2009), 808–11.

was living in Three Leg Alley just east of Fetter Lane and had a 'shopp' near St. Dunstan in the West Church, where he was an active parishioner throughout his lifetime.[180] The Marshall family has a monument in St. Dunstan's, and Marshall himself was buried there on 14 December 1675.

Marshall was especially well-known as a prolific producer of brasses, described by Sally Badham as 'the most noted seventeenth-century brass engraver'.[181] Brasses provided regular work for engravers, who often did both brass engravings and stone carvings.[182] In March of 1627, Sir Edward Dering recorded a payment to 'master Marshall' of £2 'for tombe worke in brasse', and in December of that year to 'master Marshall the tombe cutters boy' and to 'master Marshall ye tombe cutter for worke for me'.[183] In 1643–44, the churchwardens of St. Dunstan's paid Edward Marshall 'stone Cutter for altering ye inscriptions in Brasse upon Div[e]rs grave stones'.[184] His

[180] A 1641 reference described 'a Monument to bee erected in the Church for the perpetuall mamorial of the fact, which was accordingly performed by the care and labour of *Edward Marshall* Tomb-maker under St. *Dunstans* Church in the west in Fleet-street' (*A true relation of an apparition in the likenesse of a bird with a white brest, that appeared hovering over the deathbeds of some of the children of Mr. James Oxenham of Sale Monachorum, Devon. Gent.* [London, 1641], 8).

[181] Badham, *Monumental Brasses*, 18. See also Esdaile, *Temple Church Monuments*, 79; and Bertram, *Monumental Brasses as Art and History*, 5, 69.

[182] Other London marblers Nicholas Stone, Epiphany Evesham, and Frances Griggs (whose shop Marshall took over at St. Dunstan's) were all stone carvers and brass engravers (Norris, *Monumental Brasses: The Craft*, 68, 81, 82).

[183] Sir Edward Dering, 'A Book of Expenses', U350/E4, fol. 84r, Kent Archives. See Laetitia Yeandle's transcription available at https://kentarchaeology.org.uk/publications/member-publications/sir-edward-dering-lst-bart-surrendendering-and-his-booke-expences, 462 and 448.

[184] White, 'A Biographical Dictionary', 84. See also John Page-Phillips, *Palimpsests: The Backs of Monumental Brasses* (London: Monumental Brass Society, 1980), 1:22, 76. Marshall also repaired and altered the Barttelot brasses in St. Mary the Virgin, Stopham, West Sussex (Bertram, *Monumental Brasses as Art and History*, 5). See also https://sussexparishchurches.org/church/stopham-st-mary/. Herbert Haines details the extensive reforms in 1643 and 1644, including William Dowsing in Suffolk who 'destroyed 192 brasses in 52

brass to Sir Edward and Elizabeth Filmer in St Peter and St. Paul, East Sutton, completed between 1629 and 1638, has been called 'one of the finest brasses of the seventeenth century', and C.B. Newham writes that Marshall 'could also supply brasses to clients when needed'.[185] Anne Shakespeare's brass would have been part of this output.

Marshall's career can help date Anne Shakespeare's epitaph more accurately. As an apprentice to John Clarke, Marshall probably worked on building Lincoln's Inn chapel, just behind St Dunstan's churchyard.[186] Marshall completed his apprenticeship in January of 1626/27, married in June of 1627, and by 1628/29 had taken over a shop in St. Dunstan's churchyard vacated by another sculptor, Francis Grigs.[187] Since Anne's epitaph was in place no later than 1634 (when Dugdale reproduces it in his manuscript notes), a logical time frame for its creation would be after 1626/7 when Marshall finished his apprenticeship and established his workshop, and before 1634, likely by August, as it would have been customary to install a brass to commemorate the anniversary of Anne's death.[188]

A brass like Anne's would typically not be signed, so the only way to confirm attribution of the engraver is to examine similarities between the style of engraving, particularly of letter formation, since each engraver's

---

churches of that county only'. Actions included removing 'superstitious Inscriptions on the grave stones' and taking 'brasses off stones' (*Manual of Monumental Brasses*, cclvi).

[185] Newham, *Country Church Monuments*, 464.

[186] Ingrid Roscoe, 'Edward Marshall', in *A Biographical Dictionary of Sculptors in Britain, 1660–1851*, eds. Ingrid Roscoe, Emma Hardy, and M. G. Sullivan (New Haven: Yale University Press, 2009), 808–813.

[187] White, 'A Biographical Dictionary', 83–84; and Knoop and Jones, *London Mason*, 34n3. In February of 1623/24 there were seven shops in the churchyard on the street side, described in the vestry minutes as 'shops and sheds' (R. C. Bald, 'Dr. Donne and the Booksellers', *Studies in Bibliography* 18 [1965]: 70, 69–80).

[188] For the best explanation of how the apprentice system worked for early modern masons, see Ian Stone, *Crafted in Stone: A History of the Worshipful Company of Masons of the City of London* (London: Phillimore Book, 2023), 88–100.

workshop had their own individual lettering style and characteristics (much like individual handwriting), in part because of the precision required to create a monumental brass.[189] As Jon Bayliss notes, for engravers, 'the design of the lettering and the layout' were 'integral parts of the whole', so 'lettering can be used to identify individual masters of workshops who were in control of every aspect of their products'.[190] Malcolm Norris agrees that each workshop had 'particular idiosyncrasies and conventions' especially for 'the arrangement and lettering of inscriptions'.[191]

It is important to note that because brass engravings are done by hand, minor differences occur, and (as with handwriting) identical engravings are nearly impossible to produce.[192] Nevertheless, surviving visual evidence offers a convincing case for Edward Marshall's work. Anne's epitaph (Figure 16) has the following distinctive features:

1. The decorative 'H' used in the first letter of line 1
2. The numbers '162' in line 3
3. The letter 'Q' that begins line 6
4. The 'st' ligature in lines 4, 7, 8, and 9
5. The lower case 'g' in lines 6 and 7
6. The decorative flourish at the end of line 7

---

[189] See Waller, *A Series of Monumental Brasses*, iv. Norris points out that London workshops included the master craftsman as well as assistants and apprentices who carried out the established patterns of the workshop (*Monumental Brasses: The Craft*, 101). For reliance on individual lettering as the attribution method, see Page-Phillips, *Macklin's Monumental Brasses*, 40; F. A. Greenhill, *Incised Effigial Slabs* (London: Faber and Faber, 1976), and Katharine A. Esdaile, *English Church Monuments 1510 to 1840* (London: B.T. Batsford, 1946), 70.

[190] Jon Bayliss, 'Mary Howard', *Monumental Brass Society Portfolio of Brasses*, www.mbs-brasses.co.uk/index-of-brasses/mary-howard.

[191] Malcolm Norris, 'The Analysis of Style in Monumental Brasses', in *Monumental Brasses as Art and History*, 103.

[192] For details about the process of brass engraving, see Norris, *Monumental Brasses: The Craft*, 39 and Badham, *Monumental Brasses*, 13–14.

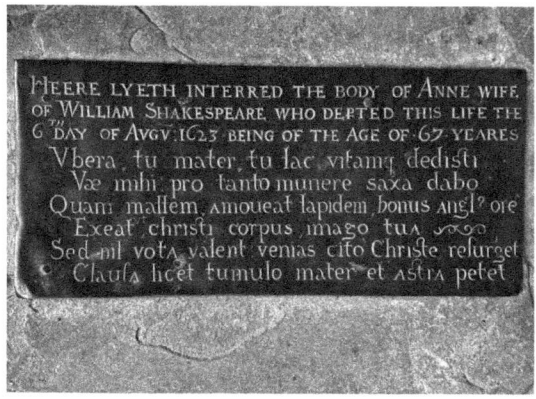

Figure 16 Anne Shakespeare's epitaph, Holy Trinity Church, Stratford-upon-Avon (author's own photo)

7. The mixture of Roman capitals and script lettering, one for lines 1–3 and a separate one for lines 4–9
8. The lower case 'l' with a side flourish, in lines 4, 6, 8, and 9
9. The lower case 'a' in lines 4–9
10. The lower case 's' with a flourish at both ends of the letter in lines 5, 6, 7, and 8
11. The connected 'HE' in lines 2 and 3
12. Capital letters 'C', 'G', and 'S' with an upward-curving hook in lines 2, 3, 8, and 9.

The 'C', 'G', and 'S' are particularly characteristic of Marshall's work.[193] Likewise, the decorative 'H' also features in Marshall's monument to Michael Drayton (discussed later in this section) and his 1641 brass for John Pen in Holy Trinity Church, Penn, Buckinghamshire.[194] The mixture of Roman capitals and script lettering appears in Marshall's

---

[193] White, 'A Biographical Dictionary', 85.
[194] Norris, *Monumental Brasses: The Craft*, plate 257.

Figures 17 and 18 Katherine Gildredge's monument, St. Mary's Church, Eastbourne, Sussex (author's own photos)

monument to Richard Braham at St. John the Baptist, Windsor; his brass to Archbishop Harsnett at Chigwell, Essex; his engraving on Sir Edward Filmer, wife and children, 1629, in East Sutton, Kent; and his 1653 monument to the Verney family at All Saints, Middle Claydon, among others.[195]

A detailed comparison of Anne's epitaph with numerous documented and signed engravings created by Marshall offers compelling evidence for Marshall as the engraver of Anne's brass. The most notable point of comparison is Marshall's signed monument to Katherine Gildredge and

---

[195] David C. Rutter, 'A Palimpsest at Little Missenden, Bucks', *Transactions of the Monumental Brass Society* 8.63 (December 1943): 47, 34–36. For details about Marshall's 1653 monument to the Verney family, commissioned by Sir Ralph Verney at All Saints, Middle Claydon, see Newham, *Country Church Monuments*, 340–1, 406.

Anne Shakespeare's Epitaph 69

Figure 19 (left) Katherine Gildredge's monument, St. Mary's Church, Eastbourne, Sussex (author's own photo); Figure 20 (right) Anne Shakespeare's epitaph, Holy Trinity Church, Stratford-upon-Avon (author's own photo)

her two children (Figures 17–19), in St. Mary's Church, Eastbourne. The monument is engraved on a slate panel and dates from 1635/36, just after the time period of Anne Shakespeare's epitaph (Figure 20).[196]

Katherine Gildredge's monument and Anne Shakespeare's epitaph (Figures 19 and 20) share almost all of Marshall's characteristics: the mixture of the same two letterform styles (reversed in Gildredge's engraving, with Roman capitals for English and script lettering for Latin); the numbers '162'; the lowercase letter 'l' with a side flourish; the lowercase 'g'; the upper case 'Q'; the decorative uppercase 'H'; the 'st' ligature; the lowercase 'a'; the number '2'; the combination of 'EST'; the double 'N'; and the decorative flourish to finish a line (see Figure 21).

---

[196] White, 'Addenda and Corrigenda', 340. Gildredge died 2 October 1629 and was buried 4 October, but her monument was not completed until 1635/6 when her daughter (also named Katherine) died. Her husband Nicholas signed the epitaph, and he was likely the impetus behind the monument's creation. I am grateful to Anne Eastbury for giving me access to photograph Katherine Gildredge's monument at St. Mary's Church, Eastbourne.

Figure 21 Side-by-side comparison of Katherine Gildredge's monument (left) and Anne Shakespeare's epitaph on the right (author's own photo)

A second signed monument by Marshall, to Henry Curwen from 1638, in St. Mary's, Amersham, also shares Marshall's characteristic mixture of lettering, as well as the hooked 'C'; the numbers 1, 6, and 3; the word 'WHO'; the word 'OF'; the ligatured 'st'; and the word 'AGE' (see Figure 22).

Anne Shakespeare's Epitaph 71

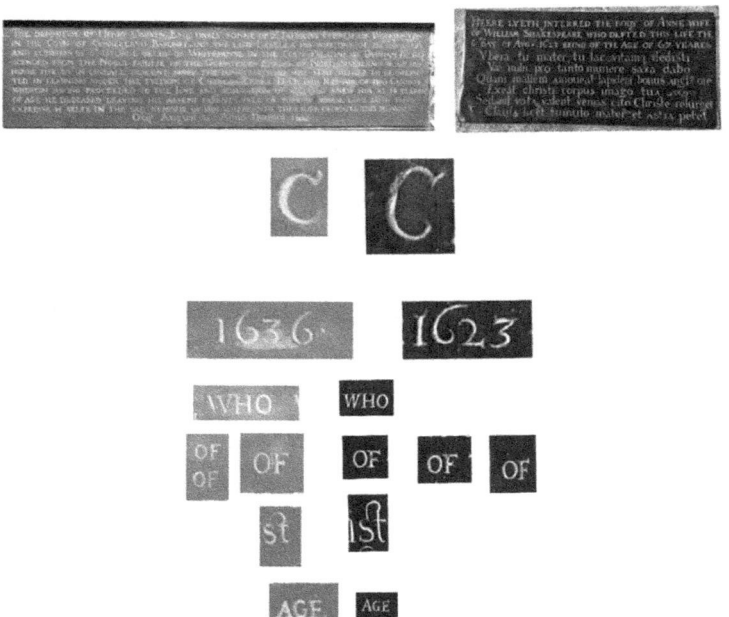

Figure 22 Side-by-side comparison of Henry Curwen's monument (left) and Anne Shakespeare's epitaph (right), Henry Curwen monument courtesy of Carolyn Gifford, https://creativecommons.org/licenses/by-nc/4.0/

The 1631 documented monument to Michael Drayton in Poet's Corner, Westminster Abbey (Figure 23) shares several features with the epitaph of Anne Shakespeare, notably the characteristic decorative 'H' used in line 1 of Anne's epitaph and in Katherine Gildredge's monument, as well as the uppercase 'AGE'; the numbers 1,6, and 3; the characteristic 'C' with a hook; the uppercase word 'OF'; the uppercase word 'THIS'; the characteristic 'S' with a hook; and the uppercase letters 'ER' (Figure 24).[197]

[197] Drayton's monument has been dated 1631 on the basis of John Stow's comment 'made in this year [1631]' (*Survey of London* [1633], 763). Drayton

Figure 23 Monument to Michael Drayton, Westminster Abbey, © Dean and Chapter of Westminster

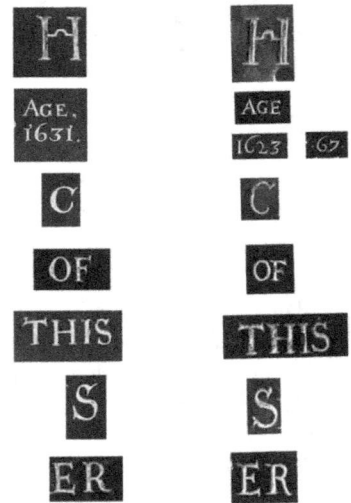

Figure 24 Side by side comparison of Michael Drayton's monument (left) and Anne Shakespeare's epitaph (right)

Anne Shakespeare's Epitaph

Figure 25 displays additional visual and letterform evidence comparing Anne's epitaph to five of Marshall's engravings.[198] Even with the uneven nature of photographic evidence, expected minor differences due to hand engraving, and the various conditions of these engravings in terms of their preservation (or lack of), the visual evidence supports the case for Marshall as the engraver for Anne Shakespeare's brass.

died in December 1631, so presumably his monument would have been completed in January or February of 1631/32 and may have been planned during his lifetime.

[198] I am grateful to Michael Bailey and the Reverend Canon Sally Lodge for giving me private access to Marshall's monuments at St. John the Baptist, Windsor, and providing additional photographs for comparison.

Anne Shakespeare (Holy Trinity Church, Stratford-on-Avon)	Michael Drayton (Westminster Abbey), 1631	Katherine Gildredge (St. Mary's Eastbourne), 1635/6	Henry Curwen (St. Mary's Amersham), 1638	Nazareth Pagett (St. John the Baptist, Windsor), 1628	Rebecca Southcot (St. John the Baptist, Windsor), 1642
 1623	 1631	1635	 1638		
 H	 H	 H			
 OF	 OF		 OF OF		 OF
 ER	 ER				
 S	 S	 S S / S S			
 C C		 C C			
 G G		 G			
 THIS	 THIS				

Figure 25 Table of comparisons between Marshall's engravings.

Anne Shakespeare's Epitaph

AGE	AGE		AGE		AGE
WHO	WHO		WHO		
g	g			g	
Q		Q			
st st		st	st		
a a		a			a
2		2		2	
EST		EST			
NN		NN			
~~		~~			

5 The Epitaph's Geography: Possible London and Stratford-upon-Avon Networks

In this final section, I put forward several possible scenarios that could explain how the Shakespeare family connected with London engraver Edward Marshall, drawing on the various social and literary connections of the Shakespeares and of Marshall.[199] Given the contemporary practice of securing such commissions through personal relationships and peer recommendations, it is unlikely that Anne Shakespeare's family would have approached Marshall without some form of personal connection.[200] It was common for families to use the same engraver for multiple memorials. However, Nicholas Johnson, the sculptor of Shakespeare's monument, had retired by 1621 and died in 1624, so the Shakespeare family would have needed to find another engraver.[201] The Halls travelled back and forth to London regularly, including one trip that Susanna Hall made to London in April 1624 with her daughter Elizabeth, the year after Anne's death.[202] It is possible that one purpose of this trip was to plan Anne's epitaph.

It is worth pointing out that we cannot completely rule out a London poet as the author of Anne's epitaph instead of her daughters, no matter how unlikely, especially since Edward Marshall was well-connected with numerous literary

---

[199] John Aubrey was a frequent visitor to Marshall's workshop and sought out Marshall for inscriptions, including an epitaph for Inigo Jones. According to Aubrey, Marshall kept records of his jobs as well as of the epitaphs he reproduced, but his materials have been lost (*Brief Lives with an Apparatus for the Lives of Our English Mathematical Writers*, ed. Kate Bennett [Oxford: Oxford University Press, 2015], 1:551, 558, 2: 1041, 1440, 1488).

[200] Choosing an engraver was determined by 'fashion, social contact ... and a strong sense of continuity within the peer group', which makes an anonymous commission doubtful (Llewellyn, *Funeral Monuments*, 187).

[201] White, 'Edward Marshall', 71. Orlin makes the argument for Nicholas Johnson as the sculptor of Shakespeare's monument in *Private Life*.

[202] In his diary for 1624, John Hall writes that 'At the beginning of April [Elizabeth] went to London,' presumably also with Susanna. See Greg Wells, *John Hall, Master of Physicke: A Casebook from Shakespeare's Stratford* (Manchester: Manchester University Press, 2020), 112.

figures of the day.[203] For example, Marshall used verses from Francis Quarles for Michael Drayton's monument; John Aubrey records: 'Mr Marshall the Stone-cutter of Fetter-lane, also told me, that these verses [on Drayton's monument] were made by Mr. Francis Quarles, who was his great Friend'.[204] As an active parishioner at St. Dunstan's, Marshall would also have known the poet John Donne, who was appointed vicar at St. Dunstan's in March of 1624 and served until his death in 1631, and who composed epitaphs, including one for his own wife. Writer James Howell left specific directions for Marshall in his will, specifying a brass and a Latin epitaph:

> I Desire my body may be carried decently in a hearse: And buried in the Middle Temple Church as privately as can be Att the ffoote of the next great Piller this side the little Quier where I have directed Mr Marshall to sett up a large Black Marble with a Brasse Picture of mine in the Middle with my Armes and a Latin Epitaph.[205]

Howell leaves no instructions for who among Marshall's circle would write his epitaph but seemed to trust that Marshall would take care of it. While it is possible that the verses for Anne's epitaph came from a London poet unconnected to the Shakespeares, the personal nature of the epitaph and its lack of recognizable conventional classical tags make this scenario highly improbable.

If we follow the line of argument that Anne's epitaph was a personal tribute, and one that could most likely only be written by someone who knew her and/or knew her family, there are several possible scenarios which might explain

---

[203] See Rutter, 'A Palimpsest at Little Missenden, Bucks', 47.

[204] Aubrey, *Brief Lives*, 1:517–18.

[205] *Epistolae Ho-Elianae: The Familiar Letters of James Howell, Historiographer Royal to Charles II*, ed. Joseph Jacobs (London: David Nutt, 1890), 669–70. Added to Howell's will is a codicil stating that 'Thirty pounds in a white Bagg which is designed for a Tomb wherein I desire my Executor to be very careful'. Katharine A. Esdaile notes, 'This brass, were it made, is no longer on the monument, which, indeed, does not seem designed to receive it: it must therefore have been placed on a lost floor slab' (*Temple Church Monuments*, 79–80).

how Marshall (based in London) connected with the Shakespeare family (based in Warwickshire). Each option I outline extends the personal and social connections of Anne and her daughters beyond the bounds of Stratford-upon-Avon, building on Matthew Steggle's contention that Anne was much more engaged in Shakespeare's social networks than has been previously thought.

Scenario 1 Marshall and the Shakespeares in Stratford-upon-Avon

It may not have even been necessary for the Shakespeare family to leave Stratford-upon-Avon in order to connect with Edward Marshall, since he was working in Holy Trinity Church in the early 1630s on the elaborate monument to the Earl of Totnes (Figure 26), recorded by Dugdale as by 'Mr Marshall in Fetter-lane', and described by the Stratford antiquarian Robert Wheler as 'a magnificent monument'.[206] George Carew became Earl of Totnes in February 1625/26 and died in March 1629. The extended Shakespeare family was linked to George Carew in the 1620s, via Susanna and John Hall's possession and inheritance of the Clopton lands in Old Stratford.[207] According to Orlin, the Totnes monument was built in 1630, when Joyce Carew had repairs done on the Clopton chest tomb in the Clopton Chapel.[208] Though the Totnes monument would likely have been completed in London and then moved to Stratford, it is possible that Marshall met the Shakespeare family while installing the monument in Stratford. Orlin suggests just such a scenario for Shakespeare and Nicholas Johnson, where Shakespeare could have 'met the tomb-maker for his old friend [John Combe] in Holy Trinity Church'.[209] Members of the Shakespeare family may have approached Edward Marshall on site and commissioned Anne's brass epitaph in person, or they could have seen his handiwork in Stratford and contacted him at a later date. Either option

---

[206] *The Life, Diary and Correspondence of Sir William Dugdale*, ed. William Hamper (London: Harding, Leopard, 1827), 99; and Robert Wheler, *History and Antiquities of Stratford* (Stratford-upon-Avon: J. Ward, 1806), 43.

[207] Mairi Macdonald, 'A New Discovery about Shakespeare's Estate in Old Stratford', *Shakespeare Quarterly* 45.1 (1994): 87–89.

[208] Orlin, *Private Life*, 200.   [209] Orlin, *Private Life*, 231.

Anne Shakespeare's Epitaph 79

Figure 26 Totnes monument to George and Joyce Carew, Holy Trinity Church, Stratford-upon-Avon, c.1630 (author's own photo)

suggests a desire to enlist a highly qualified engraver to memorialize Anne, one who had recently been employed by the most prominent family in the area. Like the connections between Anne's epitaph and Dean Balsall's tomb, linking Anne's epitaph to Marshall's work for the prominent Clopton family would have been another way to underline Anne's social position in Stratford.

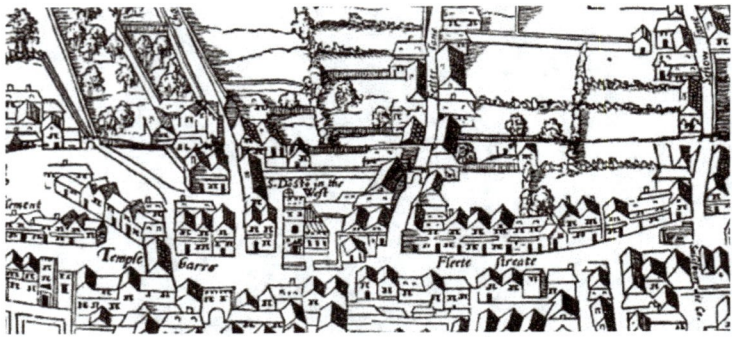

Figure 27 'Plan of London (circa 1560 to 1570)', in Agas Map of London 1561 (1633) British History Online https://www.british-history.ac.uk/no-series/london-map-agas/1561/map

Scenario 2 A Mutual Acquaintance: Michael Drayton, Edward Marshall, and the Shakespeares

Michael Drayton had close connections with the Shakespeare family in Stratford-upon-Avon, and with Edward Marshall in the London literary community. Between Anne's death in 1623 and Drayton's in 1631, could he have served as an intermediary between the two parties? Such a relationship would suggest a widespread respect for Anne Shakespeare among mutual friends in her husband's literary and social circle. When Marshall created Drayton's monument in Westminster Abbey, he would have known Drayton personally since they were close neighbours as well as fellow parishioners at St. Dunstan's. According to John Aubrey, Drayton 'lived at the bay-windowe house next the East-end of St. Dunstans Church in Fleetstreet' (Figure 27) very close to Marshall's workshop on Fetter Lane; the geography of London around St. Dunstan's is still remarkably similar to the Agas map in Figure 27.[210]

---

[210] Aubrey, *Brief Lives*, 1:517.

Aubrey records that the Countess of Dorset 'gave [Drayton's] monument. This Mr. Marshall (the stone-Cutter) who made it, told me so'.[211] Drayton was a sociable figure, described as 'of an honest life and upright conversation', and he had many connections in the same social circles as Marshall. The antiquary William Fulman recorded that Drayton died 'not rich; but so well beloved, that the Gentlemen of the Four Innes of Court and others of note about the Town, attended his body to Westminster, reaching in order by two and two, from his Lodging almost to Standbridge'.[212]

Drayton and Shakespeare probably knew each other through a social network of friends from Stratford at Middle Temple and may have even shared poetry in manuscript.[213] The Inns of Court were connected with the St. Dunstan's literary community, and two of the printers at St. Dunstan's, Nicholas Ling and John Smethwick, printed works by both Drayton and Shakespeare. Six of Drayton's 25 known plays (of which only one is preserved) are connected to Shakespeare's work, and it has been suggested that he 'modeled himself on Shakespeare in part because of their shared background'.[214] Even after Shakespeare's death, Drayton continued his connections with Shakespeare's works and with the Shakespeare family. He almost certainly owned a copy of the First Folio, since, according to Andrew Hadfield, he made closer reference to Shakespeare's works after 1623.[215] Drayton probably bought his Folio at St. Dunstan's, where some of his own works were printed, and his

---

[211] Aubrey, *Brief Lives*, 1:517. Aubrey incorrectly attributes Drayton's monument to Anne Clifford, instead of her sister-in-law Mary Countess of Dorset. See Bernard H. Newdigate, *Michael Drayton and His Circle* (Oxford: Shakespeare Head Press, 1961), 221.

[212] Francis Meres, *Palladis Tamia: Wits Treasury* (London: P. Short, 1598), 281, quoted in Newdigate, *Michael Drayton and His Circle*, 219.

[213] Meghan C. Andrews, 'Michael Drayton, Shakespeare's Shadow', *Shakespeare Quarterly* 65.3 (2018): 289, 293–297. For other connections between Shakespeare and the Inns of Court, see Lois Potter, *The Life of William Shakespeare: A Critical Biography* (London: Wiley-Blackwell, 2012), 92, 151–6.

[214] Andrews, 'Michael Drayton', 274–5, 284.

[215] Andrew Hadfield, 'Michael Drayton's Brilliant Career', *Proceedings of the British Academy* 125 (2004): 140. See also Newdigate, *Michael Drayton and His Circle*, 140–1.

strong ties to the St. Dunstan's community could easily have led to the production of Anne's epitaph on behalf of his Stratford friends.

As well as being a close friend of Edward Marshall, Drayton also had several personal and professional connections to the Shakespeare family. Both Drayton and Shakespeare were from Warwickshire, born in the 1560s, and like many Stratfordians in London, both maintained their Warwickshire ties throughout their lifetimes. According to one account, Stratfordians in London 'would have found it difficult to escape the dense social networks which characterize small-town life', including 'a fairly efficient network of Stratford gossip in London'.[216] Susan Brock describes Drayton's Stratford-upon-Avon life as 'part of a social circle which overlapped with Shakespeare's' and notes that Drayton 'visited for some months every summer to rest and to write'.[217] Paul Edmondson and Stanley Wells note that Drayton's ties with the Rainsford family in the nearby village of Clifford Chambers 'suggest that both he and Shakespeare may often have been in the area at the same time, possibly discussing their work with each other'.[218] In his *Poly-Olbion* (1612), Drayton referred to 'deere Cliffords seat (the place of health and sport)/Which many a time hath been the Muses quiet Port'. If Stratford vicar John Ward's apocryphal account of Shakespeare's death is to be believed, 'Shakespeare, Drayton, and Ben Jonson had a merry meeting and it seems drank too hard, for Shakespeare died of a fever there contracted'.[219] Even though Ward's account of Shakespeare's death is impossible to verify, there is a grain of truth to the friendship and social connections between Drayton and Shakespeare, making it possible that Drayton also knew Anne personally. Drayton's relationships with the Shakespeare family were extensive; he was a patient of Anne's son-in-law John Hall, who described him as 'an excellent Poet', and he thus likely knew Susanna Hall.[220] Linking

---

[216] Hope and Wright, 'Female Education', 149–50.

[217] Susan Brock, 'Last Things: Shakespeare's Neighbours and Beneficiaries', in *The Shakespeare Circle*, 218.

[218] Paul Edmondson and Stanley Wells, 'Closing Remarks', in *The Shakespeare Circle*, 333.

[219] *The Notebook of John Ward, 1662–1663*, fol. 150r, V.a.292, Folger Shakespeare Library.

[220] Greg Wells, *John Hall, Master of Physicke*, 95–96.

Scenario 3 Anne's Lodgers and the London Legal World: Thomas and Lettice Greene

Thomas and Lettice Greene lived with the Shakespeares at New Place in Stratford from roughly 1603 to 1610/11, and had close personal relationships with the Shakespeare family, as well as professional and literary connections in both London and Stratford-upon-Avon. In his diary, Thomas referred to himself as Shakespeare's 'cosin', evidence of a close relationship rather than kinship; Lettice had perhaps an even closer relationship with Anne.[221] Thomas Greene was Shakespeare and Drayton's closest acquaintance at Middle Temple, and Middle Templar Sir Henry Rainsford was also on friendly terms with Greene, Drayton, Shakespeare, and John Hall.[222] Anne and her daughters were likely connected with all of them.

While there is no direct evidence to connect the Greenes with Edward Marshall, they often circulated with many of the same acquaintances. Thomas Greene spent a large portion of his professional career in Stratford-upon-Avon but maintained his connections with the Inns of Court and with the literary community there throughout his lifetime. Greene entered Middle Temple in 1595, and Paul Edmondson speculates that he may have even seen the first recorded performance of Shakespeare's *Twelfth Night* in February 1602 at Middle Temple.[223] In 1602 Greene was called to the bar, and by 1603, he had moved to Stratford. It may have been Shakespeare's connections with the Inns

---

[221] Paul Edmondson, Kevin Colls, and William Mitchell, eds. *Finding Shakespeare's New Place: An Archaeological Biography* (Manchester: Manchester University Press, 2016), 110–1; Tara Hamling, 'His "cousin" Thomas Greene', in *The Shakespeare Circle*, 135–7. Germaine Greer conjectures that 'Ann and Thomas and Lettice Greene must have enjoyed each other's company, having lived under the same roof for so long' (*Shakespeare's Wife*, 284).

[222] Andrews, 'Michael Drayton', 296–7.

[223] Edmondson, *Finding Shakespeare's New Place*, 111.

of Court that brought Greene to Stratford.[224] He served as town clerk until his resignation in 1617, the year after Shakespeare's death, when the Greenes moved to Bristol. By the 1620s Greene had resumed activity at Middle Temple, within the time frame that Anne's epitaph was created.[225]

The Greenes were well connected with many of the Shakespeares' relatives and associates in Stratford. Along with Shakespeare's lawyer Francis Collins, Greene witnessed Thomas Combe's will in 1608, and Collins would later take over from Greene as town clerk in 1617. In 1611, Lettice Greene, Thomas Greene, and Judith Shakespeare Quiney served as witnesses for Elizabeth Quiney's sale of a house in Wood Street. Greene was a fellow trustee with John Hall in 1613 for Richard Lane, and Thomas Greene's brother John was a lawyer of Clement's Inn and a trustee of the Blackfriars Gatehouse in 1618, acting on behalf of Susanna Hall. Thomas Greene served with Anne's kinsman Richard Hathaway on the Stratford Council from 1615 until 1619.[226] It is clear that the Greenes' connections to the wider Shakespeare family were far more extensive than those of typical lodgers.

Further, Anne Shakespeare and Lettice Greene's lives would have intersected closely in the eight years they both lived at New Place, from 1603 (the year the Greenes probably married) until 1610/11, paying rent which Anne likely collected.[227] As Paul Edmondson points out, New Place had 'plenty

---

[224] For the many connections between Shakespeare, Stratford, and Greene at the Inns of Court, see Christopher Whitfield, 'Some of Shakespeare's Contemporaries at the Middle Temple', *Notes and Queries* 13.4 (1966): 122–5; 13.8 (1966): 283–7; 13.10 (1966): 363–9; 13.12 (1966): 443–8.

[225] Robert Bearman, ed., *Minutes and Accounts of the Corporation of Stratford-upon-Avon and Other Records*, Vol. 7, 1610–1620 (Bristol: The Dugdale Society, 2022), 14–19; Edmondson, *Finding Shakespeare's New Place*, 114; and John Taplin, *Shakespeare's Country Families: A Guide to Shakespeare's Country Society with Appendices and Genealogies* (Warwick: Claridges, 2018), 125.

[226] Bearman, *Minutes and Accounts*, 31–32.

[227] Robert Bearman, 'Thomas Greene: Stratford-upon-Avon's Town Clerk and Shakespeare's Lodger', *Shakespeare Survey* 65 (2012): 295. Edgar I. Fripp and Peter Ackroyd suggest Greene may have been living with the Shakespeares as early as 1601 (*Shakespeare: Man and Artist*, 2:543; and Ackroyd, *Shakespeare: The Biography* [London: Chatto and Windus, 2005], 474). See also

of space for Greene and his family, and it can easily be imagined that they lodged very comfortably in perhaps a set of two or three rooms that formed part of one of the wings'.[228] In September 1609, Thomas Greene wrote that he 'mighte stay another yere' at New Place, which suggests a positive experience. The Greenes had moved nearby to their own lodging of St. Mary's by June 1611 but maintained ties with the Shakespeares, witnessing the sale of a property by Elizabeth Quiney (along with Judith Shakespeare) in December of that year. The Greene's daughter Elizabeth was born the following June 1612, likely named after Susanna and John Hall's four-year-old daughter Elizabeth.

When the Greenes lived at New Place, the women – Anne, her daughters Susanna and Judith, Lettice Greene, and perhaps Anne's mother-in-law Mary Arden Shakespeare – would have experienced several key life moments in the same household, including births, weddings, and deaths. As a mother of three, Anne Shakespeare likely offered counsel and advice on childbirth and motherhood. Her epitaph's eulogy as a beloved mother may reflect not only her own experience, but also her support of her daughters and other community women, in what Adrian Wilson calls the 'ceremony of childbirth'.[229] For most early modern women, childbirth was 'one of the ways in which women were embedded in their families and communities', a social occasion for women to bond in a community without men, and a ritual that was both female and collective.[230]

Seventeenth-century surgeon Robert Barret recommended that the birthroom should include the midwife along with 'some sober, wise Women, among her Neighbours, such as have gone through the like hazard before'.[231]

Christopher Whitfield, 'Thomas Greene: Shakespeare's Cousin. A Biographical Sketch', *Notes and Queries* 11.12 (1964): 442–455. On Greene's absence in Shakespeare's will, see Potter, *William Shakespeare*, 404, 290–305.

[228] Edmondson, *Finding Shakespeare's New Place*, 112.

[229] Adrian Wilson, *Ritual and Conflict*, 153. See also Wilson's discussion of the female communal experience of childbirth in 'Participant or patient? Seventeenth-century childbirth from the Mother's point of View', in Roy Porter, ed., *Patients and Practitioners: Lay Perceptions of Medicine in Pre-industrial Society* (Cambridge: Cambridge University Press, 1986).

[230] Gowing, *Common Bodies*, 156.

[231] Robert Barret, *A Companion for Midwives* (London: Thomas Axe, 1699), 7.

Married women who were experienced in childbirth took part in other women's childbirths, and the communal experience would have extended through the subsequent month-long lying-in period, when 'the women who attended the birth would stay for "good cheer" and would return periodically with others for gossiping and good fellowship'.[232] The anonymous satirical pamphlet *The Batchelars Banquet* (1603) describes a scene of female sociability where 'every day after her lying down will sundry dames visit her, which are her neighbours, her kinswomen, or other her special acquaintance'.[233] As Adrian Wilson describes it, 'the collective ritual of childbirth was an integral part of a wider women's culture', and the rituals of childbirth and lying-in were 'effectively universal' among married mothers.[234]

Several babies were born to the women at New Place under Anne's watch, and the women in residence there – Anne, Lettice Greene, Susanna Shakespeare, and Judith Shakespeare – would have engaged in the female collective rituals connected to the birth process. The first baby born in New Place was Lettice Greene's daughter Anne in March 1604 (baptized on 18 March). The fact that Lettice likely named her child after Anne Shakespeare suggests that Anne's New Place was a supportive environment for her.[235] As women of the household, both Susanna (age twenty-one) and Judith (age nineteen) may have prepared the traditional drink of mother's caudle or darkened the room and prepared candles.[236] The Shakespeare women at New Place would have been the first visitors to Lettice during her lying-in

---

[232] Cressy, *Birth, Marriage, and Death*, 58, 84.

[233] *The Batchelars Banquet* (London, 1603), 14. See also the scene in Thomas Middleton's play *The Chaste Maid in Cheapside*, discussed by Gail Kern Paster in *The Body Embarrassed*, 52–63. Other scholarly works on the collective female experience in childbirth include Sara D. Luttfring's *Bodies, Speech, and Reproductive Knowledge in Early Modern England* (London: Routledge, 2016) and Caroline Bicks's *Midwiving Subjects in Shakespeare's England* (Aldershot: Ashgate, 2003).

[234] Wilson, *Ritual and Conflict*, 156, 179.

[235] For a less optimistic interpretation of the supportive communal experience of childbirth, see Gowing, *Common Bodies*, 149–76.

[236] I have relied on Adrian Wilson's description of the social processes of childbirth in *Ritual and Conflict*, 153–210.

period, when the 'celebratory, collective female character of the birth was continued into the process of lying-in', and they would have been the ones to accompany Lettice (along with her midwife) to church at the end of the lying-in period.[237] The Shakespeares could have been the godparents or sponsors for baby Anne at her baptism ceremony in Holy Trinity Church.[238] This would explain Thomas Greene's frequent references to Shakespeare as his 'cosin', a close relationship that could also entail serving as a godparent.

As a woman who had experienced maternal grief, Anne Shakespeare could also have been a source of comfort for Lettice Greene when she buried her unnamed infant child on 3 August 1606, just ten years after Anne experienced the loss of her only son Hamnet in 1596, and again in March of 1610 when the Greenes had another infant daughter who did not survive. Avra Kouffman comments that women often felt the loss of a child was 'a measure of God's justice', and were 'plagued with guilt and shame', and Anne might have sympathized with the guilt that Lettice may have felt.[239] The following year, in 1607, Lettice would have been part of the more celebratory household preparations for the marriage of Susanna Shakespeare to John Hall in June.

In 1608, both Lettice Greene and Susanna Hall gave birth to children at New Place. Lettice's son, appropriately named William, was baptized on 17 January, and Susanna's daughter Elizabeth was baptized a month later on 21 February.[240] Lettice and Susanna would have experienced their pregnancies in tandem, and their young children would have grown up together in New

---

[237] Wilson, *Ritual and Conflict*, 173. Women would have been accompanied by other women, often the same ones who had attended the birth.

[238] Wilson records that the parents typically 'had no place in the baptism ceremony; the parents' place was taken by the god parents or "sponsors"' (*Ritual and Conflict*, 173).

[239] Avra Kouffman, 'Maternity and Child Loss in Stuart Women's Diaries', in Kathryn M. Moncrief and Kathryn R. McPherson, eds. *Performing Maternity in Early Modern England* (Aldershot: Ashgate, 2007, 173). Elizabeth Walker lost all 11 children, and wrote about every 'sweet Child, and dearly beloved' in her spiritual diary *The Holy Life of Mrs. Elizabeth Walker* (1690). See Kouffman, 'Maternity and Child Loss', 175–9, 171–182.

[240] Taplin offers an alternative explanation for the naming of the Greene children. See *Shakespeare's Country Families*, 134.

Place. They may even have used the same midwife. The female community at New Place when William and Elizabeth were born in early 1608 would also have included Anne's mother-in-law Mary Arden Shakespeare, who would die later that year in September. It is logical to think that Anne's maternal role was formative to some degree for all of the women who resided in New Place.

Lettice Greene may have learned more than the skills of motherhood from Anne Shakespeare. St. Mary's, the Greenes' home, was described in 1617 as having a 'brewing furnace and a brewhouse, as well as some land'.[241] Since Anne likely ran the brewing business at New Place, it stands to reason that she would have been the one to instruct Lettice in the practice of ale brewing.[242] There is a high probability that Lettice Greene was literate; when she signed the property deed for Elizabeth Quiney, she used an italic hand and her 'ink distribution is even and her hand confident'.[243] She could also apparently read. In January 1614, William Chandler wrote to Thomas Greene at Middle Temple, 'I would intreate you if you have not the note of Remembrance that you tooke concerninge Mr Combe and other busyness at London all ready, then I would intreete you to Right downe to my mother greene that shee may send you the note up to you in the next retorne of the carrier.'[244] Hannah Lilley points out that Lettice could read her husband's 'fiendishly tricky cursive handwriting' and could 'navigate her husband's working space to the point of locating a particular document'. She was thus also entrusted with her husband's business dealings at Middle Temple and at Stratford.[245] The next year, in 1615, Lettice provided key information to her husband related to the Welcome enclosures: Greene writes that 'at night at my Commyng home my wif told me yt was sayd while we were as at the

---

[241] Hannah Lilley, 'Lettice Greene of Stratford-upon-Avon and Her World', *Middling Culture: The Cultural Lives of the Middling Sort, Writing and Material Culture, 1560–1660* (14 August 2020), https://middlingculture.com/2020/08/14/lettice-greene-of-stratford-upon-avon-and-her-world/.

[242] Orlin, 'Anne by Indirection'. [243] Lilley, 'Lettice Greene'.

[244] BRU15/5/151, Shakespeare Birthplace Trust Archives.

[245] Lilley, 'Lettice Greene'. See also Bearman, 'Thomas Greene', 305; and *Minute and Accounts*, 474, 477, 494, 500, 666.

Assises'.²⁴⁶ Did Lettice Greene, a literate and trusted woman, help contribute to the memorialization of a key maternal figure in her life?

The fact that the Greenes maintained ties with the Halls, who would also have been living in New Place until 1613 when they moved to Hall's Croft, increases the likelihood of a sustained familial relationship. In 1614, a local enclosure dispute brought Greene together with Shakespeare and John Hall. When Greene sold his house in Stratford in 1617, part of the money was delivered 'to mr Hall at Newplace'.²⁴⁷ The Greenes' time at Stratford must have been a positive experience since Greene referred to his time in Stratford as his 'golden days' in a letter of May 1617.²⁴⁸ When Anne Shakespeare died in 1623, Thomas and Lettice Greene would have been in a position to connect the Shakespeares with the Inns of Court community, the St. Dunstan's literary circles, and possibly Edward Marshall. Lettice may have even advised Susanna and Judith on the depiction of Anne as a beloved mother who expressed her spirituality through her 'duty' of breastfeeding.

Another compelling point in favour of the Greenes' role in Anne's epitaph is the eight-line Latin poem Thomas Greene wrote in his diary from December 1614, when his wife Lettice was about to give birth. Greene's poem includes a familiar *ars moriendi* theme: 'Death is certain, uncertain the day, the hour known to none; think therefore any day to be thy last.'²⁴⁹ In

---

[246] Shakespeare Birthplace Trust, BRU15/13/26a. See *Shakespeare Documented*, https://doi.org/10.37078/494.

[247] Mark Eccles, *Shakespeare in Warwickshire* (Madison: University of Wisconsin Press, 1961), 129. See also Bearman, *Minutes and Accounts*, 14–19.

[248] Fripp, *Shakespeare's Stratford*, 60.

[249] BRU15/13/26a, Shakespeare Birthplace Trust Archives. Marlin E. Blaine has pointed out that Greene's poem is appropriated from other sources. 'Latin Culture', forthcoming. For the *ars moriendi* trope, see *The Death Arts in Renaissance England: A Critical Anthology*, eds. William E. Engel, Rory Loughnane, and Grant Williams (Cambridge: Cambridge University Press, 2022), 5–14. Greene's poem is quoted in full and translated by Fripp in *Shakespeare's Stratford*, 59–60. See also Stanley Wells, 'Greene, John and Thomas', *The Oxford Companion to Shakespeare*, eds. Michael Dobson and Stanley Wells (Oxford: Oxford University Press, 2001), 173. See Robert Bearman, 'Thomas Greene's Notes on the Progress of the Proposed Enclosures

his will of 1641, Greene referred to his wife as 'so good a woman', and he clearly valued her role as a wife and mother.[250] Could this maternal respect have contributed to the maternal accolades in Anne's epitaph?

One final connection between the Greenes, the Shakespeares, and the London literary world is through Michael Drayton. Thomas Greene knew Michael Drayton from Middle Temple and the two had several literary connections.[251] Greene dedicated a poem to Drayton, which appeared in Drayton's 1603 collection *The Barron's War*s. Drayton and Greene also had a mutual friend in Henry Rainsford, who Greene knew from Middle Temple and Drayton knew from Clifford Chambers.[252] The scenario I have presented in this section posits a network of relationships that links the extended Shakespeare family with their Stratford connections and with the wider literary community through Thomas and Lettice Greene, and these ties may have facilitated the memorial of a beloved maternal figure and friend.

Scenario 4 St. Dunstan in the West's Literary Sphere: A Context for Anne Shakespeare's Epitaph

One of the most intriguing options for how Anne and her family became associated with Edward Marshall is through the literary community of St. Dunstan in the West and its neighbouring legal district. The location of Marshall's shop and the surrounding community connected with the publication of Shakespeare's texts suggest a close connection between the Shakespeare family in Stratford and the London literary world. Edward Marshall's shop was located in the heart of the St. Dunstan's publishing community, and Marshall had close friendships with many of the printers and booksellers there, most of whom were

---

at Welcombe Include Five References to William Shakespeare's Involvement', *Shakespeare Documented*, https://doi.org/10.37078/494.

[250] Eccles, *Shakespeare in Warwickshire*, 130.

[251] J. William Hebel, *The Works of Michael Drayton* (Oxford: Shakespeare Head Press, 1961), 5: xxiii, xxiv, 53, 55, 66, 69, 180, 281, 28–8, 292.

[252] Edmondson, *Finding Shakespeare's New Place*, 111; Bearman, 'Thomas Greene', 292; and Taplin, *Shakespeare's Country Families*, 134.

Anne Shakespeare's Epitaph 91

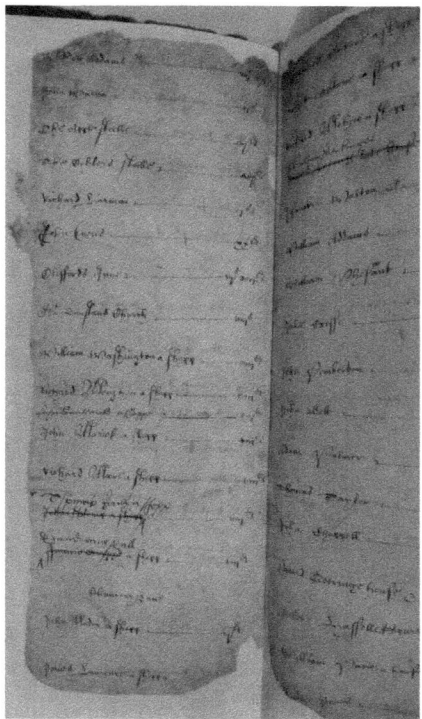

Figure 28 1629 Scavengers' rate assessments, St. Dunstan's Churchyard, London Archives, by permission of the Guild Vicar and Churchwardens of St. Dunstan-in-the-West. Image courtesy of Ben Higgins.

also active parishioners.[253] In 1629, a surveyor recorded a list of shops in the churchyard of St. Dunstan's (Figure 28), which provides

[253] Marshall may also have been familiar with the name of Shakespeare from advertisements of his plays, since a typical Londoner would know about theatre performances 'through reading the advertisements hanging on the posts of London', and separately printed title pages were 'so present and so numerous that it was hard for the casual observer not to read them'. Shakespeare's name began to appear on a regular basis on title pages after 1597 (Tiffany Stern,

a snapshot of St. Dunstan's around the time that Anne Shakespeare's epitaph was created.[254]

> William Washington a Shopp
> Richard Meighen a Shopp
> John Smithwick a shoppe
> John Mariott a Shopp
> Richard Moore a Shopp
> \Thomas Jones a shopp/
> ~~John Stemp a Shopp~~
> \Edward Marshall/
> ~~Francis Grigge~~ a Shopp

The name of Francis Grigg is crossed out, since Marshall took over his shop that year. A second survey the following year in 1630 (Figure 29) lists a similar array of shops.

> \George Smithwick/
> ~~William Washin~~ton a shopp
> Richard Meighen a shopp
> John Smithwicke a shopp
> John Mariott a shopp
> Richard more a shopp
> Thomas Jones a shopp
> Edward Marshall a shopp

The other six shops listed were occupied by bookselling publishers connected with Shakespeare's works, putting Marshall's shop in the heart of what Ben

Documents of Performance in Early Modern England [Cambridge: Cambridge University Press, 2009], 37, 48).

[254] Franz Kellendonk's description of the shops as 'sheds' suggests an even close proximity of inhabitants (*John and Richard Marriott: The History of a Seventeenth-Century Publishing House* [Amsterdam: Polak and Van Gennep 1978], 5).

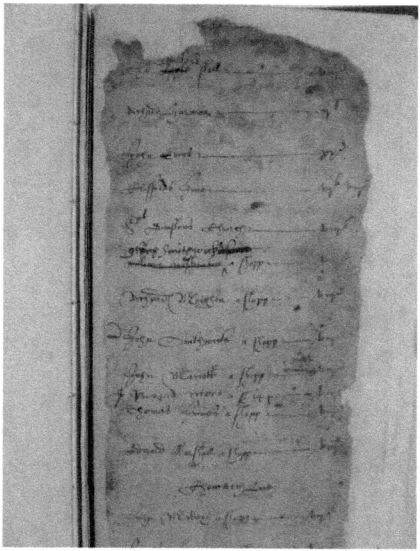

Figure 29 1630 Scavengers' rate assessments, St. Dunstan's Churchyard, London Archives, by permission of the Guild Vicar and Churchwardens of St. Dunstan-in-the-West. Image courtesy of Ben Higgins.

Higgins has called 'the home of Shakespeare publishing' in the late 1620s and 1630s and nicknamed by R.C. Bald as 'little St. Paul's'.[255] St. Dunstan's continued to be a key site for the printing of Shakespeare's texts as late as the 1640s; John Benson published his 1640 edition of Shakespeare's *Poems* from his shop 'in St. Dunstans Church-yard'. Figure 30 shows a later layout of St. Dunstan's along Fleet Street, which probably resembled the shops in the earlier seventeenth century.

[255] Ben Higgins, *Shakespeare's Syndicate: The First Folio, Its Publishers, and the Early Modern Book Trade* (Oxford: Oxford University Press, 2022), 204; and Bald, 'Dr. Donne', 69. See also Jennifer M. Young, 'Minding Their F's and Q's: Shakespeare and the Fleet Street Syndicate 1630–32', *Historical Networks in the Book Trade*, eds. John Hinks and Catherine Feely (London: Routledge, 2017), 83–100.

Figure 30 William Henry Toms, c. 1700–c. 1750, The Southeast Prospect of the Church of St. Dunstan in the West, 1737, Engraving, Yale Center for British Art, Paul Mellon Collection, B1977.14.15927.

According to Marta Straznicky, even passers-by would know the wares of a shop, since they would have had 'a stall out front or a hinged board projecting from the wall where books could be displayed'.[256] As someone who would have passed by these shops on a regular basis, Edward Marshall could scarcely avoid the Shakespearean wares of his fellow tenants. A closer look at the booksellers

[256] Marta Straznicky, 'Shakespeare in the Early Modern Book Trade', in *The Arden Research Handbook of Shakespeare and Textual Studies*, ed. Lukas Erne (London: Arden Bloomsbury, 2021), 122. See also Peter W. M. Blayney, *The Bookshops in Paul's Cross Churchyard* (London: The Bibliographical Society, 1990), 10–11, 94–116

shops and the books that would have been for sale at St. Dunstan's underlines the likelihood that Marshall would have known the Shakespeare name.

Richard Meighen, the publisher of Ben Jonson's 1616 Folio, owned two bookshops, one in the churchyard of St. Dunstan's and the other opposite Middle Temple gate, and is listed in both scavengers' rate assessments for 1629 and 1630 (Figures 28 and 29). Meighen was one of the financiers of the 1632 Shakespeare Folio, along with William Aspley, Robert Allot, Richard Hawkins, and John Smethwick, another of the St. Dunstan's stationers. Meighen sold the second edition of the Shakespeare Folio in 1632 and the 1630 quarto of *The Merry Wives of Windsor* (Figure 31) from his shop next to the gate to Middle

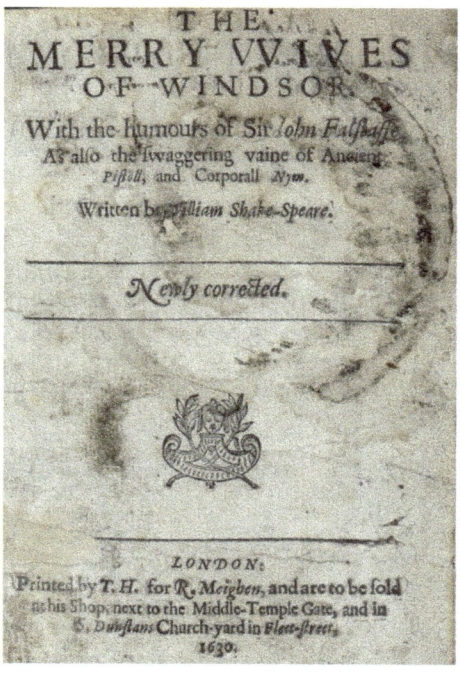

Figure 31 *The Merry Wives of Windsor* (1630), title page to the third quarto, A1 recto, Folger Shakespeare Library STC 22301

Temple, where his directive was to 'sell books for students of the law'.[257] The proximity of Meighen's shop in particular, and the whole literary community of St. Dunstan's to the Inns of Court, may have given him close connections with people like Thomas Greene, who circulated between London and Stratford.[258]

John Marriott, a bookseller whose shop was also listed on both scavengers' rate assessments, was a close friend of Edward Marshall. Marriott described the 'marbler' Marshall in his will of November 1660 as 'my assured loving and most kind friend', bequeathing him 20*s* to 'buy him a ring to weare in memory of his poore friend', and 20*s* more to Marshall's wife 'to buy her a small ringe in memorie of their love and great kindness which I have constantly received from them, for which I pray God to blesse them and there children'.[259] In addition to the close proximity of their businesses, Marriott lived in the parish of St. Dunstan's in the West all of his life. He had a shop on Fleet Street near Fetter Lane, at the sign of the White Flower-de-Luce, and probably took over John Smethwick's shop 'under the dial' when Smethwick died in 1641.[260] Marriott held several offices in the Stationers' Company and was the publisher from 1618 for the Royal College of Physicians, and later for a number of authors. He published John Donne's 1633 *Poems*, and 16 editions of poet Francis Quarles's work, from 1629 until 1644; Quarles, as we have seen, was also a friend of Marshall's.[261] Marriott published the second part of Michael Drayton's *Poly-Olbion* in 1622, with John Grismand. As a publisher of Drayton, Marriott could have enlisted his close friend Marshall to commemorate Anne for their mutual friend Michael Drayton.

A third St. Dunstan's publisher, John Smethwick, offers another avenue for connecting the Shakespeare family networks to the London literary milieu. Smethwick was a long-standing bookseller and publisher of Shakespeare's

---

[257] Higgins, *Shakespeare's Syndicate*, 187.

[258] Laoutaris discusses the proximity of St. Dunstan's to the Inns of Court in *Shakespeare's Book*, 127–32.

[259] Kellendonk, *John and Richard Marriott*, 10.

[260] Kellendonk, *John and Richard Marriott*, 4, 7.

[261] Higgins, *Shakespeare's Syndicate*, 146n65.

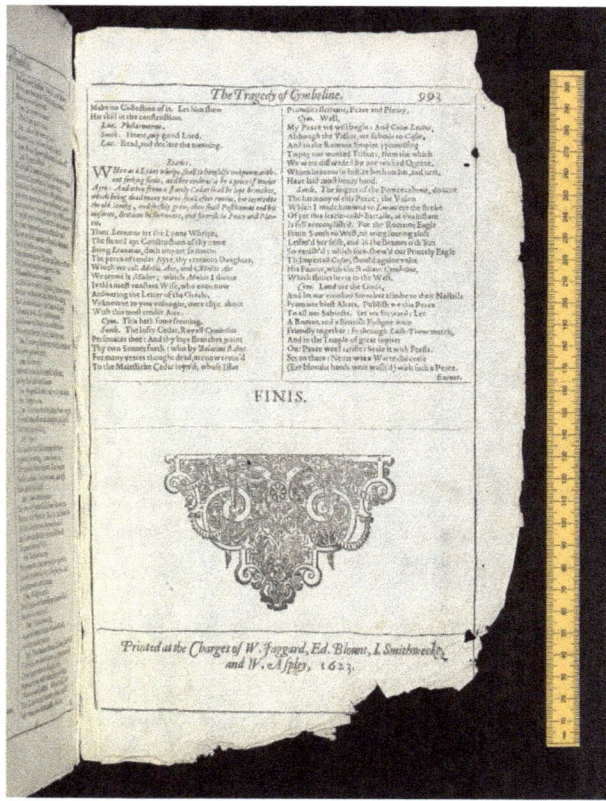

Figure 32 William Shakespeare, *Mr. William Shakespeares comedies, histories, & tragedies*. London: Printed by Isaac Jaggard and Edward Blount for William Jaggard et al., 1623 (sig. bbb6r), Bodleian Library, Arch. G c.7 (CC BY)

writing. He is listed in the colophon of the First Folio (Figure 32) and held the publishing rights to four Shakespeare plays: *Romeo and Juliet*, *Hamlet*, *Love's Labour's Lost* (Figure 33), and *The Taming of the Shrew* (Figure 34). Ben

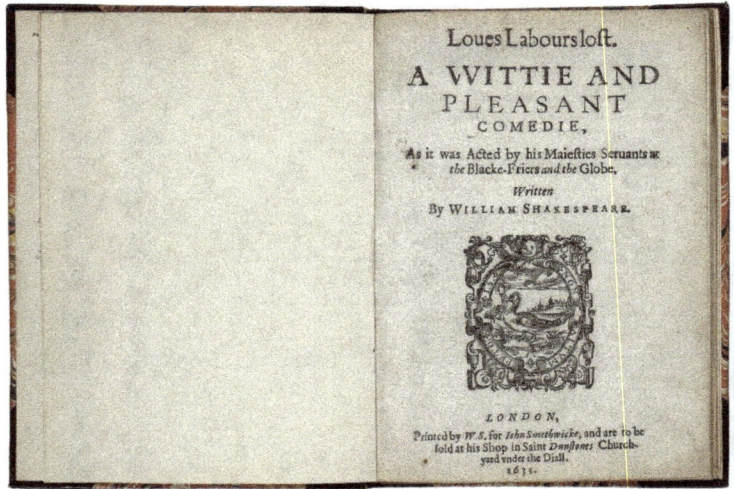

Figure 33 Title page to the 1631 quarto of *Love's Labour's Lost*, A1 recto, Folger Shakespeare Library

Higgins describes Smethwick as 'the most significant stakeholder with whom the Folio syndicate had to negotiate when it came to assembling the volume in the early 1620s' (Figures 33 and 34).[262] From his shop 'under the Dial' of the clock at St. Dunstan's, Smethwick played a major role in the distribution of Shakespeare's plays through the 1630s, and was involved in the publication of the second Folio in 1632 (Figure 35), making him a key figure connected to the Shakespeares.[263] Chris Laoutaris speculates that Smethwick 'would have

---

[262] Higgins, *Shakespeare's Syndicate*, 172. Smethwick held the rights to *The Taming of A Shrew* which passed to him along with *Love's Labour's Lost* and *Romeo and Juliet* on 19 November 1607 following the death of Nicholas Ling. But the proprietorial rights to publish *A Shrew* (and potential loss of capital should *Th Shrew* appear) were almost certainly sufficient for Smethwick to assert rights to publication for the alternative version.

[263] Andrew Murphy, *Shakespeare in Print: A History and Chronology of Shakespear Publishing* (Cambridge: Cambridge University Press, 2003), 51–53.

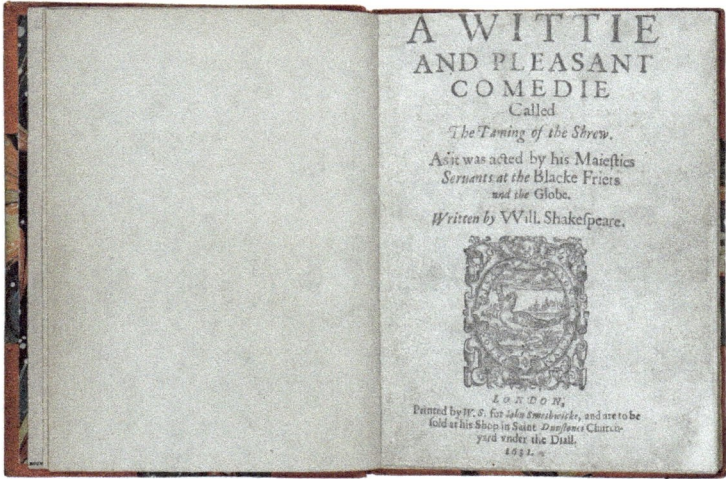

Figure 34 Title page to the 1631 quarto of *A Wittie and Pleasant Comedie Called The Taming of the Shrew*, A1 recto, Folger Shakespeare Library

provided a list of contacts in the St Dunstan's vicinity which may have proved helpful in the negotiations for the Folio's plays'. He also catered to the law students at the Inns of Court and 'arranged copies on his own shelves' of the First Folio 'where they could attract the legal set who worked or studied at the nearby Inns of Court and the area's other legal institutions'.[264] Did Smethwick's display of the Shakespeare Folio catch the eye of Thomas Greene, who had returned to the Inns of Court by the 1620s, may have heard of the recent death of Anne Shakespeare, and sought out an esteemed engraver to commemorate her for her family?

Smethwick knew Edward Marshall, not only because of the close proximity of their shops, but also as fellow active parishioners at St Dunstan's. Smethwick was elected constable in 1619, became a junior

---

[264] Laoutaris, *Shakespeare's Book*, 131, 281–2.

Figure 35 William Shakespeare, *Mr. William Shakespeare's Comedies, Histories, and Tragedies*. London: Printed by Thomas Cotes, for John Smethwicke, 1632, A2 recto, Folger Shakespeare Library

churchwarden in 1627 and a senior churchwarden in 1628, which entitled him to a new pew in the chancel, for which he paid the vicar 6 *s.* 8 *d.*[265] When Edward Marshall moved to the parish of St Dunstan's in late 1628 or early 1629, John Smethwick would have been the parish churchwarden, having just paid John Donne to preach an Easter sermon there in 1628.[266] Smethwick also knew Michael Drayton as fellow parishioners at St. Dunstan's, and was the publisher for several of his works, including his 1619 folio. Did the close-knit web of Smethwick, Drayton, and Marshall relate to the commission of Anne's epitaph? The plausibility of such connections increases significantly given Matthew Steggle's recent persuasive argument that William and Anne Shakespeare shared both a London residence (likely around 1599–1603) and social and business networks.[267]

Around the time of Anne's death, the Shakespeare name would have been familiar to several other booksellers in the area who sold his works. William Jaggard's shop was at the east end of St. Dunstan's churchyard, and his brother John was a bookseller on Fleet Street near St. Dunstan's. William Jaggard died in November 1623 and his business was taken over by his son Isaac, who became printer to the City upon his father's death.[268] Further evidence suggests a close friendship between the Jaggards and John Smethwick. Chris Laoutaris remarks that Smethwick and John Jaggard became particularly close due to their work in the parish of St. Dunstan's, and both families both baptized children and buried loved ones in the church, so 'the two families were closely affiliated'.[269] Ben Higgins has pointed out similarly that Smethwick was close to the Jaggard family because they shared parish duties – both Smethwick and John Jaggard served as parish constables in 1619 and 1620.[270] Two more booksellers, William Sheares and Richard Hawkins, had shops just outside of St. Dunstan's, at Serjeant's Inn, nearby to where Marshall later moved at Whitefriars stairs.

---

[265] Bald, 'Dr. Donne', 70. [266] Higgins, *Shakespeare's Syndicate*, 171.
[267] Steggle, 'The Shakspaires of Trinity Lane'.
[268] Straznicky, 'Shakespeare in the Early Modern Book Trade', 113.
[269] Laoutaris, *Shakespeare's Book*, 130. [270] Higgins, *Shakespeare's Syndicate*, 203.

Sheares sold the 1632 quarto of *I Henry IV* and Hawkins sold the 1630 quarto of *Othello*.

Situated amidst the hub of Shakespeare publishing, Edward Marshall must have recognized the Shakespeare name when he received the commission for Anne's epitaph. The intricate web of relationships between the printers and booksellers of Shakespeare's texts at St Dunstan's, the connections of Greene and Drayton to the area and to the Shakespeare family, and Marshall's central location within this network, strongly suggest a more long-standing relationship between the Shakespeares and the London literary scene.

Scenario 5 A Convivial Connection to Anne's Epitaph: Ben Jonson, Edward Marshall and the Devil Tavern

Readers will recall the posthumous anecdote from Stratford vicar John Ward discussed earlier, that Ben Jonson and Michael Drayton held a 'merry meeting' just before Shakespeare's death in Stratford. I have suggested that both Drayton and Jonson may have known Anne from such encounters (provided they are more than apocryphal). Through Edward Marshall, it is possible to link Jonson and Drayton to a wider literary network that maintained ties to the extended Shakespeare family well after Shakespeare's death. One of the landmarks of the neighbourhood surrounding St. Dunstan in the West was the Devil Tavern, located between Middle Temple Lane and Temple Bar, where Ben Jonson regularly gathered in the 1620s with the 'Tribe of Ben', including Michael Drayton, Robert Herrick, Richard Brome, Thomas Randolph, and James Howell, among others.[271] Their favoured location was the Apollo Club room on the second floor, which had a musician's gallery,

---

[271] Kellendonk makes this suggestion in *John and Richard Marriott*, 19–20. See also Katharine Esdaile, 'Ben Jonson and the Devil Tavern', *Essays and Studies* 29 (1943): 93–100; Michelle O'Callaghan and Adam Smyth, 'Tavern and Library: Working with Ben Jonson', *Essays and Studies* 62 (2009): 155+; and Richard Harp, 'Ben Jonson: Madness and Community', in *Community-Making in Early Stuart Theatres*, eds. Anthony W. Johnson, Roger D. Sell, and Helen Wilcox (London: Routledge, 2017), 240–1.

wall hangings, a seat for Ben Jonson, and a bust of Apollo.[272] Drayton pays homage to the Apollo Club room in his 1619 ode 'The Sacrifice to Apollo'.[273] An inscription of 30 November 1620 in a copy of Drayton's *Poems* from 1619, given to Richard Butcher 'by the authors hande', further links Drayton to the space: 'Written at the Devell/& St Dunston in the/poets hall called Apollo'. In his inscription, Butcher refers to spending 10 shillings at the command of Drayton 'In sack & smoke to cheare his merry muse'.[274] Jonson praised Drayton in his tribute to Drayton's 1627 folio as the writer of 'pure, and perfect *Poesy*' and it has been suggested that Jonson later wrote the epitaph for Drayton's monument in Westminster.[275]

Edward Marshall possibly carved the bust of Apollo in the Devil Tavern, due to the proximity of his shop to the space and to his friendship with many of the frequenters of the Devil, including Michael Drayton and James Howell, whose monuments Marshall created.[276] A further connection between Marshall and Jonson is the famous Latin tavern code *Leges Convivales* that Jonson wrote for their meetings, which was 'engraved in gold letters on a marble tablet over the mantelpiece'.[277] In a letter of

---

[272] David Riggs, *Ben Jonson: A Life* (Cambridge, MA: Harvard University Press, 1989), 285; and Esdaile, 'Ben Jonson and the Devil Tavern', 94.

[273] See Newdigate, *Michael Drayton and His Circle*, 138.

[274] John Buxton, 'The Poets Hall Called Apollo', *The Modern Language Review* 48 (1953): 53.

[275] R. W. Short, 'Ben Jonson in Drayton's Poems', *Review of English Studies* 16.62 (1940): 149–58. Aubrey attributes Drayton's epitaph to Francis Quarles, as I discussed earlier.

[276] Esdaile, 'Ben Jonson and the Devil Tavern', 100. This attribution has been challenged; see Fran C. Chalfont, *Ben Jonson's London: A Jacobean Placename Dictionary* (Athens: University of Georgia Press, 2008), 67n5.

[277] Percy Simpson, 'Ben Jonson and the Devil Tavern', *The Modern Language Review* 34 (1939): 367–73. Marshall may have completed other engravings for Ben Jonson. Michelle O'Callaghan and Adam Smyth note that 'Jonson even had an epigram he made for Robert Cecil, Earl of Salisbury, in praise of his father, William, Lord Burleigh, engraved on a gold plate that was probably presented as a New Year's gift' ('Tavern and Library', 165).

19 June 1624, John Chamberlain wrote to Sir Dudley Carleton, 'I send here certain *Leges convivales* of Ben Johnsons made for a faire roome or chamber lately built at the tavern or signe of the divell and St. Dunstan by Templebarre: they be reasonable goode and not improper for such a place'.[278] If Marshall was responsible for the bust of Apollo, it seems likely that he also engraved Jonson's tavern code on the marble tablet, linking him more closely to Jonson in the decades after Shakespeare's death.

It is compelling to think that Anne Shakespeare might have been part of the literary and social networks of her husband through one or more of the scenarios that I have outlined. Given Marshall's many connections to numerous friends of the Shakespeare family and his shop's proximity to the heart of Shakespeare publishing, it is plausible that his production of Anne's memorial stemmed from these long-standing links between the Shakespeare family – not just William Shakespeare – to literary London.

Conclusion: Expanding the World of Anne Shakespeare

If we connect Anne Shakespeare to the literary world of early modern London, what might that tell us about her? For one, such connections might link her to the production of the 1623 Folio.[279] The King's Men travelled to Stratford in the summer of 1622, a year before Anne's death, and they may have visited Anne, perhaps in search of Shakespeare's papers to use as copy texts. As a close colleague and friend of Shakespeare (one of three beneficiaries from the King's Men in Shakespeare's will), John Heminges may have even known Anne. It is possible that the commemoration of Anne in a plaque likely engraved by Edward Marshall stemmed from long-standing personal relationships between Anne and the literary and theatrical personnel who may have visited her in 1622 to obtain Shakespeare's manuscripts and that the production of her epitaph may have been connected to her role

---

[278] *The Letters of John Chamberlain*, ed. N. E. McClure (Philadelphia: The American Philosophical Society, 1939), 2:566.

[279] See Greer, *Shakespeare's Wife*, 345–6, 352–6; and Fripp, *Shakespeare Man and Artist*, 2:852.

in the Folio.[280] The production of Anne's epitaph by Edward Marshall, 'writ in brass', as Ben Jonson's Folio poem describes the printed portrait of her husband, may have been a further tribute, organized not only by family, but also by personal friends of her family.

However Anne Shakespeare's epitaph came to be produced by Edward Marshall, it seems clear that Marshall would have known exactly who he was commemorating when he began to engrave the lines 'Heere lyeth interred the body of Anne wife of William Shakespeare', a beloved mother and 'so great a gift' to her community. Until further evidence comes to light, it is impossible to say which of the scenarios I have outlined is the most likely one, but each provides a broader picture of Anne Shakespeare, one that extends her reach beyond Stratford and connects her much more closely to the literary world of seventeenth-century London. The networks of production for her epitaph suggest that those connections endured even in her later years, and that her daughters had multiple avenues to pursue when they sought to commemorate her.

***

The year 2023 was the 400th anniversary both of the First Folio and of the death of Anne Shakespeare. In January of that year, I visited her grave in Stratford-upon-Avon to take photos for this project. In an empty church (and with special permission), I was able to see the minute traces of Edward Marshall's carving to make permanent the tribute from her daughters Susanna and Judith and to imagine the power that their words would have held when immortalizing their mother so long ago in the shadows of the wall monument to their father, as if he were looking on, as he still is. A few days

---

[280] Laoutaris suggests that the January 1624 performance of *The Winter's Tale* at Whitehall, which took place less than six months after Anne's death, may have been a form of 'monumentalized motherhood', a tribute to the wife of a close friend, and perhaps even a personal friend. *Shakespeare's Book*, 257–8. Laoutaris notes that a 'John Hemynge' was a witness for the will of Anne's father Richard Hathaway in 1581. If the Folio's John Heminges is from the Shottery family, he would have been one of the seven Heminges children baptized at Holy Trinity in Stratford between 1563 and 1582 (257).

later, I travelled to Eastbourne on a bitterly cold and rainy day to see Katherine Gildredge's monument in a deserted St Mary the Virgin Church. The lower quarter of the monument is just about eye level, making it easy to photograph the bottom part and even to trace the engraving with my own fingers. Marshall's signature is still visible at the bottom of that monument. When seen in person, it is obvious that these two commemorations are a match and were engraved by the same hand. It was a profoundly moving experience for me, having travelled across the ocean from Minnesota, to see these two engravings within the space of a few days. Both are commemorations of mothers, separated by only a few years in life but by 200 miles in distance, one in the Midlands and the other in East Sussex on the south coast, now united by the knowledge of their common engraver.

It is especially poignant to see Edward Marshall's own monument to his three young children, which I now visit every time I am in London. It is located in the old St. Dunstan in the West Burial Ground, just off of Bream's Buildings, a space frequently encroached upon by construction works and new development, and increasingly 'being worn away from memory' and 'scoured blank by time'.[281] Barely legible are the names and dates of Marshall's three children who all died around the time of Anne Shakespeare's epitaph – his second son Samuel, who died at age 2 in May 1631; his eldest daughter Anne who died at age 1 in June 1635; and his third son Nicholas, who died in December 1635, age 5. I wonder if Marshall was grieving his own young children as he carried out the memorial to express the grief of Anne's daughters.

In honour of the 400th anniversary of Anne Shakespeare's death in 2023 a number of initiatives brought Anne to the fore of Shakespeare commemorations as a woman in her own right. The publication of the first poetry anthology for Anne – *Anne-thology: Poems Re-Presenting Anne Shakespeare* (edited by Paul Edmondson, Aaron Kent, Chris Laoutaris, and myself) - centred Anne in a series of sixty-seven newly commissioned poems, one for each year of her life. Additionally this collection for the first time brought together the historical poetry related to Anne, including William Henry

---

[281] Ross, *A Tomb with a View*, 76.

Ireland's 1796 'Verses to Anne Hathaway', Mathilde Blind's 1894 sonnets in honour of Anne written while she was in residence in Stratford-upon-Avon, and Charles Dibdin's 'A Love Dittie', with the commonly repeated refrain, 'She hath a way,/Anne Hathaway'. For the first time, Anne's epitaph was printed with Susanna Shakespeare Hall and Judith Shakespeare Quiney listed as the authors. The Shakespeare Birthplace Trust sponsored a competition among students at Shakespeare's school, King Edward VI school, to set an English translation of Anne's epitaph to music. The winning anthem, composed by student Ariana Pethard, premiered at the Shakespeare's Birthday weekend service on 23 April 2023, when Paul Edmondson delivered a sermon for Anne as part of the celebrations of her famous husband's birthday. On Sunday, 6 August 2023, 400 years to the date of Anne's death, I delivered the first sermon in her honour at Holy Trinity Church, just steps from the epitaph that is the subject of this Element. There has been a sermon in honour of Shakespeare delivered at Holy Trinity every year since the nineteenth century, but until 2023, never an annual sermon in honour of Anne.

As I complete this Element to reanimate the maternal 'Anne' that her daughters almost certainly had a hand in immortalizing, her epitaph endures, steadfastly testifying across time to the shared human experiences of grief, motherhood, and strength, deeply embedded in a space where Anne herself once knew both hope and anguish, joy and grief. Susanna and Judith could scarcely have foreseen the centuries of misogyny that Anne would face in her afterlife, ranging from the dismissal of the beautiful original Latin poetry as 'six lines not worth remembering', to her denigration as a 'disastrous mistake' of a wife in a prominent twenty-first-century biography. Even so, it is gratifying that the choices Susanna and Judith made 400 years ago – employing a top sculptor, using brass, opting for a chancel burial, and crafting a Latin epitaph – will continue to immortalize the 'gift' of their mother.

Appendix: An Edition of Anne Shakespeare's Epitaph

Heere lyeth interred the body of Anne wife of William Shakespeare, who dep[ar]ted this life the 6th day of Aug[ust] 1623, being of the age of 67 yeares.

Vbera, tu mater, tu lac vitamque dedisti	1
Væ mihi: pro tanto munere saxa dabo	2
Quam mallem, amoueat lapidem, bonus angelus orem	3
Exeat, ᵛᵗ christi corpus, imago tua	4
Sed nil vota valent: venias citò Christe, resurget	5
Clausa licet tumulo mater et astra petet.	6

You, Mother, gave [your] breasts, milk, and life;	1
Woe is me: in return for so great a gift I shall give rocks	2
How I'd prefer, I would pray, that the good angel should move the stone away	3
[And] out would come, like the body of Christ, the image of you!	4
But prayers are of no avail: come quickly, Christ, she shall rise again	5
[My] mother, although she has been shut in the tomb, and she shall seek the stars.	6

The opening line in the English section, 'Heere lyeth', was the most conventional way to begin an epitaph. It signals not only the place of Anne's body, but also the significance of the location.

1. Vbera is a bold opening to the epitaph, but the reference to Anne as a breastfeeding mother links her to a long tradition of virtuous and pious women.
2. 'Woe is me': Simon Watney points out that 'explicitly Puritan epitaphs rarely include references to tears or personal sorrow of any kind' and had 'prevailing Puritan hostility to any displays of

Appendix

mourning that could be deemed to be intercessions on behalf of the faithful departed, and hence in Puritan terms superstitious' ('Sky Aspiring Pyramids', 111). The motif of Anne as a gift recurs in lines 1 and 2 with repetition of 'dedisti' and 'dabo'.

3. Line 3 is rendered 'bonus angelus orem': Dugdale and Chambers also read this as 'orem'.

3–4. Victoria Moul has pointed out the thematic focus on the alteration/contrast between the subjunctive in lines 3–4 (what I wish would happen but won't) vs the future indicative (what *will* happen), which juxtaposes the fantasy of Anne coming back to life now vs. the reality of faith in the final resurrection.

4. The added superscript 'vt' is in the original and Victoria Moul suggested that this was likely a mistake of Edward Marshall's rather than in the original, since it is a basic error which is not compatible with the level of Latinity in the piece as a whole.

5–6. 'Rise again': The final image of Anne's epitaph is the central Christian theme of resurrection, though 'et astra petet' does not explicitly refer to heaven.

6. 'Tumulo' also appears in John Hall's Latin epitaph. See 'His Daughter Susanna Hall', 79–80.

Acknowledgements

This Element began as an invited talk for the 2023 Shakespeare's Birthday conference at the Shakespeare Institute, organized by Paul Edmondson. I am grateful to him for the opportunity to sketch out an initial version of the argument which I have expanded here. Many other people helped refine my argument and aided my thinking about the significance of Anne's epitaph, including Sheila Cavanagh, Ailsa Grant Ferguson, Ewan Fernie, Chris Laoutaris, Laurie Maguire, Nabil Matar, Andrew Scheil, Tiffany Stern, and John Watkins. Ben Higgins generously shared material from his work on printer John Smethwick, as well as copies of the scavengers' rate assessments. Victoria Moul offered expert advice on the Latin translation and transcription, as well as the context for early modern Latin. Ian Stone kindly shared his book on the history of the masons. In making the arguments in this Element, I offer special thanks to Robert Bearman for his expertise on the Shakespeare graves; to Lena Cowen Orlin, whose magisterial work *The Private Life of William Shakespeare* (Oxford: Oxford University Press, 2021) opened multiple avenues for further research; and to the expert on engravers in this period, Adam White, who generously reviewed my evidence about Anne's epitaph and agreed with my conclusions regarding the engraver Edward Marshall. Matthew Steggle and Laurie Maguire read earlier drafts of this project and offered solidarity as well as important forthcoming work, as did Marlin Blaine. The series editors, Claire Bourne and Rory Loughnane, as well as Emily Hockley, have been incredible champions of the project from the start. I am grateful to the anonymous readers for the press for their support and encouragement.

Visual components are crucial to my argument in this Element, and several people have been essential in helping me to procure photographs and other illustrations. Paul Edmondson helped with photographs of Anne's epitaph and the Totnes monument in Holy Trinity Church. Mike Bailey gave me a personal tour of St John the Baptist Church in Windsor and provided extensive photographic evidence from Edward Marshall's monuments there. John Vigar kindly shared photographs, and Anne Eastbury a

St Mary the Virgin, Eastbourne, provided access to Katherine Gildredge's monument.

This Element is dedicated to Paul Edmondson and to Sir Stanley Wells, whose enduring friendship and unwavering support over the years have been 'so great a gift'.

Cambridge Elements ≡

Shakespeare and Text

Claire M. L. Bourne
The Pennsylvania State University

Claire M. L. Bourne is Associate Professor of English at The Pennsylvania State University. She is author of *Typographies of Performance in Early Modern England* (Oxford University Press 2020) and editor of the collection *Shakespeare / Text* (Bloomsbury 2021). She has published extensively on early modern book design and reading practices in venues such as *PBSA*, *ELR*, *Shakespeare*, and numerous edited collections. She is also co-author (with Jason Scott-Warren) of an article attributing the annotations in the Free Library of Philadelphia's copy of the Shakespeare First Folio to John Milton. She has edited Fletcher and Massinger's *The Sea Voyage* for the *Routledge Anthology of Early Modern Drama* (2020) and is working on an edition of *Henry the Sixth, Part 1* for the Arden Shakespeare, Fourth Series.

Rory Loughnane
University of Kent

Rory Loughnane is Reader in Early Modern Studies and Co-director of the Centre for Medieval and Early Modern Studies at the University of Kent. He is the author or editor of nine books and has published widely on Shakespeare and textual studies. In his role as Associate Editor of the New Oxford Shakespeare, he has edited more than ten of Shakespeare's plays, and co-authored with Gary Taylor a book-length study about the 'Canon and Chronology' of Shakespeare's works. He is a General Editor of the forthcoming

Oxford Marlowe edition, a Series Editor of Studies in Early
Modern Authorship (Routledge), a General Editor of the
CADRE database (cadredb.net), and a General Editor of The
Revels Plays series (Manchester University Press).

ADVISORY BOARD

Patricia Akhimie
The Folger Institute
Terri Bourus
Florida State University
Dennis Britton
*University of British
  Columbia*
Miles P. Grier
*Queen's College,
  City University
  of New York*
Chiaki Hanabusa
Keio University
Sujata Iyengar
University of Georgia
Jason Scott-Warren
University of Cambridge

M. J. Kidnie
University of Western Ontario
Zachary Lesser
University of Pennsylvania
Tara L. Lyons
Illinois State University
Joyce MacDonald
University of Kentucky
Laurie Maguire
*Magdalen College, University
  of Oxford*
David McInnis
University of Melbourne
Iolanda Plescia
Sapienza – University of Rome
Alan Stewart
Columbia University

ABOUT THE SERIES

Cambridge Elements in Shakespeare and Text offers a platform for original scholarship about the creation, circulation, reception, remaking, use, performance, teaching, and translation of the Shakespearean text across time and place. The series seeks to publish research that challenges–and pushes beyond–the conventional parameters of Shakespeare and textual studies.

Cambridge Elements ≡

Shakespeare and Text

ELEMENTS IN THE SERIES

Shakespeare, Malone and the Problems of Chronology
Tiffany Stern

Theatre History, Attribution Studies, and the Question of Evidence
Holger Schott Syme

Facsimiles and the History of Shakespeare Editing
Paul Salzman

Editing Archipelagic Shakespeare
Rory Loughnane and Willy Maley

Shakespeare Broadcasts and the Question of Value
Beth Sharrock

Shakespeare and Scale: The Archive of Early Printed English
Anupam Basu

Textual Genealogies and Shakespeare's History Plays
Gary Taylor and John V. Nance

Anne Shakespeare's Epitaph
Katherine West Scheil

A full series listing is available at: www.cambridge.org/ESTX

For EU product safety concerns, contact us at Calle de José Abascal, 56–1°, 28003 Madrid, Spain or eugpsr@cambridge.org.

www.ingramcontent.com/pod-product-compliance
Lightning Source LLC
LaVergne TN
LVHW021948060526
838200LV00043B/1956